Born and raised in Scotland, Anton Hodge has spent his working life in England, much of it on the border between the two countries. During that time he indulged his passion for local history, writing two books about the area and wasting many a weekend trudging around castles, battlefields and museums, before his eldest son persuaded him to start watching Gretna football club instead. Now living in North Yorkshire, Anton can be contacted through via www.antonhodge.co.uk and @antonhodge.

IN BLACK AND WHITE

The Rise, Fall and Rebirth of Gretna Football

ANTON HODGE

Chequered Flag PUBLISHING

First published in the UK by Chequered Flag Publishing
PO Box 4669, Sheffield, S6 9ET
www.chequeredflagpublishing.co.uk

A CIP record for this book is available from the British
Library

Printed in the EU by Print Group Sp. z o.o.

ISBN 9780993215230

I would like to dedicate this book to three groups of important people.

Firstly to all of those who made Gretna FC such an astonishing experience, especially Ron and Helen MacGregor, Rowan Alexander and Davie Irons, and of course to the generosity and kindness of Brooks Mileson and his son Craig.

Secondly to those who have made Gretna FC 2008 what it is today, with particular note to Craig Williamson, Sandra Bowdon and Stuart Rome. Pete George's hard work at the beginning should also be remembered. There are many others – too numerous to put down everyone's name here – but you know who you are, and you'll probably find yourself somewhere in the following pages.

Finally, to my two boys: Leon, for being driven around the country, sitting patiently, never complaining, occasionally looking up from his book or magazine to give a cry of 'Come on Gretna!'; and Rufus, for his assistance in the early days, for being chief ballboy, for painting and tidying Raydale, stuffing envelopes and so on – but mostly just for helping to start the adventure.

Introduction

'Where did they come from?'

It's Saturday 13 May 2006, my thirty-seventh birth-day, and I am sitting in the East Stand at Hampden Park awaiting the start of the 121st Scottish Cup Final. Next to me is my eight-year-old son Rufus; two friends, Pete and Graeme; and Graeme's wife Gill; all of us wearing the black and white scarves of Gretna FC, the tiny football miracle from the border where England and Scotland clashed for centuries. Today the opponents are Edinburgh's Heart of Midlothian, who have just finished as runners-up in the Scottish Premier League, a full two leagues above Second Division Gretna.

Gretna are the underdogs. We support a team which have, so the detractors say, only made it to the final by avoiding top flight opposition. The fact that we have had to defeat four First Division sides en route is conveniently forgotten. There are many critics with my team in their sights, although very few of them are here today at Hampden. We are surrounded by thousands of fellow Gretna fans, most of them singing along to the clumsy cup song: 'Living the dream we always wanted… It doesn't get any better than this.'

Down below us on the pitch, as kick-off approaches, stands Rowan Alexander, currently the longest-serving football manager in Scotland, resplendent in full Highland dress, a sprig of heather sprouting from his lapel. Alexander has been in charge at Gretna for six years and must be thinking back to the early days when the team played in front of crowds of fifty or so people in non-league games in the north of England. In those times he spent most of his waking hours (some say his sleeping hours too) at Raydale Park, the club's ramshackle ground for nearly sixty years, cutting the grass, lining the pitch, painting the walls. These days, he stays clear of the groundsman's hut and can mainly be found in offices at the club, using state of the art software to analyse the performances of his team and those of our opponents.

Almost four years ago, a dishevelled ponytailed millionaire who lives locally had begun to invest in Gretna and urged Alexander to decide whether to be a full-time caretaker or a full-time manager. Since then Alexander and the insurance magnate Brooks Mileson, his grey ponytail shining in the Hampden sun, have struck up a partnership which, they declare, will never die. It has provoked a mixture of emotions in friend and foe alike: fear, jealousy, admiration and joy.

'Where did *they* come from?' Rufus asks me again. He is referring to the Gretna-supporting crowds that embrace us with their good humour and alcoholic laughter, all 12,000 of them. The last game we had attended, three weeks ago, had attracted 2,201 supporters – a larger-than-average crowd who came along to watch captain Chris Innes being presented with the league trophy. It was a fair question: the population of Gretna (if you include the adjoining Gretna Green) stands at 2,705. Even when embellished by those of us who lived outside the town but within Gretna's self-declared catchment area (we lived eight miles away over the border), the crowd was spectacularly huge. The question was not asked with any hint of possessiveness. It was good to be part of the big crowd for once, even if it was possible by checking out the varying states of anxiety (or lack of it) to ascertain which of those in the crowd genuinely cared for the club and which were here just for a day out with nothing to lose.

But it was also a question about Gretna itself. Where *had* this tiny club come from, and how on earth did it find its way here to the Scottish Cup Final, with European competition guaranteed for next season, only four years after playing in non-league football in England? The answer mainly lay down below us in the figures of Alexander and Mileson. Although the story of Gretna FC had started just after the Second World War, it was only these last few years which had seen unprecedented success – not just in Scottish football terms, but also in a way beyond these shores. Where indeed had they come from?

This book attempts to tell the story of football in Gretna in modern times. It starts with the forming of Gretna FC in 1946 and tracks how the club became a solid component of the non-league system in the north of England, arguably achieving better than might be expected of such a small club. The next stage began with election to the Scottish Football League in 2002. The book follows the inexorable rise through the leagues to Hampden and beyond.

Fast-forward two years after the Scottish Cup Final: Rufus, Pete, Graeme and I were once again spending my birthday watching Gretna play Hearts. This time we were spectators at the last ever game played by the club. Following what the last chairman of Gretna FC, would call its 'rise and rise' came the spectacular self-combustion of the club in the spring of 2008.

The next few weeks and months would be spent in a flurry of action group and committee meetings, public presentations, debate and argument, business plans and research, telephone calls, emails, TV, radio and press interviews, meetings with MPs, MSPs, councillors and representatives from other football clubs, and the occasional clandestine rendezvous in a hotel bar. For my birthday after that, I would – as chairman of the new

Gretna football club – receive a card signed by the entire squad, coaching and other staff.

These were tricky times, but there is a happy ending. This book also deals with the resurrection of football in the town, with the new club, and explains just how all that came about and how we came to be involved in the project to raise something from the dead.

1

As you cross the border into Scotland from Cumbria, the first town you encounter is Gretna. On the right-hand side is Gretna Gateway Outlet Village where designer clothes can be picked up at bargain prices, directly ahead is the (technically separate) village of Gretna Green, famous for its eloping couples and blacksmiths. To the left is the main road which takes you through the regimentally built housing, ending in the main shopping nucleus (a bank, a baker, takeaway shops, grocery shops, wedding shops, an insurance company – its windows plastered with football regalia), and out past the greyhound racing track towards Annan. Before you get to the dog track, however, a long thoroughfare known as Dominion Road turns sharply left and extends almost down to the shore of the Solway. Partway down this road lies a sizeable chunk of vacant ground where the Sunday market now struggles to compete with the cut-price goods available almost everywhere else and a harsh brick building plays host to the Gretna Social and Athletic Club. This land is called Raydale and standing opposite the social club is a football ground which has stood there since 1947, only narrowly avoiding destruction a few years ago.

There have been three senior football clubs in Gretna. The first had been around in the nineteenth century but went bust in the 1920s. The second, Gretna Football Club, was formed in 1946 by a group of local businessmen, schoolteachers and soldiers newly returned from the war. Chief among these were the chemist James Mitchell and shopkeeper Jock Kerr, who, along with Jock's two recently demobilised brothers and five others, each provided £10 – the equivalent of around £385 nowadays – to start things moving. As an ex-player for, amongst others, Blackburn Rovers and Brentford, Jock had some practical experience, but decided to seek the advice of Dumfriesbased Queen of the South on how to run a football club. The new team immediately joined the Dumfriesshire Junior League where they remained for one season only, finishing third behind close neighbours Annan Athletic.

During that first season, home games were played at Station Park, also known as Mackie's Field, just to the north of the village and near to the railway line. To the west of Gretna, the area of land which would later become Raydale had been owned by the Ministry of War and been host to a hospital. This land changed hands a number of times before half of it was sold just after the Second World War to the trustees of the new football club.

Unlike its fellow border town on the east coast, Berwick-upon-Tweed, Gretna has not had to endure the turmoil of being passed between England and Scotland over the years; in Berwick's case this happened some thirteen times before it became English on a permanent basis in 1482. Walking around Gretna, however, and especially sitting in the stand at Raydale Park, the mixture of English and Scottish accents and language (and the language is often quite interesting at Raydale) emphasises that the border starts exactly where Gretna does, at the River Sark which joins the Solway Estuary flowing out to the Irish Sea.

After that first year in the Dumfries League, the young Gretna Football Club transferred 'into' England and joined the Carlisle and District League. The land at Raydale had cost £200 (£7,700 nowadays) and the club soon began preparing it for use, assisted by German and Italian prisoners of war who were waiting to be sent home. Gretna won their first game in the new league in their new ground, beating Holme Head 4-2. The season went well for the club, finishing second in the table and winning the League Cup. It was an indicator of how, from the very start, the team, which played even then in black and white hoops, would become one of the strongest in the area. During the thirty-four seasons up to 1982 that Gretna competed in the Carlisle and District League, the team were champions twenty times; in most seasons at least one trophy found itself wearing the Gretna team ribbons. There was one missing season: in 1951-52, Gretna played in the more geographically spread (and supposedly higher standard) Cumberland County League in its inaugural season, finishing second. That league folded after one season due to the higher costs incurred by clubs being unsustainable.

Financially the club appears to have coped too, helped very much by the new social club which was first opened in 1958. In 1963, the trustees bought the remaining land to the north (also for £200, although by now this was worth around half of what it had been in 1946). It was on this land that the second social club was built in 1970 – further evidence of the financial strength of the club – and where the Sunday market was held. The market opened in 1973 but was short-lived, and it wasn't until 1980 that it was resurrected, becoming popular and fairly lucrative. It survives today although to say it is a shadow of its former self is understating even that cliché.

Buoyed by financial and footballing success, when the chance came to join a larger league, Gretna jumped at it.

The Northern League in England is the second oldest in the world, having been founded in 1889. For nearly a century it survived as an amateur competition within the overall Football Association setup, alongside professional leagues such as the English Football League and, from 1968, the Northern Premier League (no relation). In 1979 the pyramid feeder system began, whereby the Alliance Premier League (with many subsequent name changes) began a promotion/relegation arrangement with the Football League (into Division 4 as it was then), although the clubs still had to be officially elected by the Football League – something which was denied every champion until 1987, when automatic promotion was brought in. The Northern Premier League became a feeder to the Alliance Premier League and has remained so. For whatever reason, those at the helm of the Northern League decided not to be part of the new pyramid at first and it was not until 1991 that a decision was taken to join, feeding into the Northern Premier.

Gretna's opportunity came in 1982 when the Northern League created a second division – the tenth tier of the football pyramid – and advertised for applicants. The team from Scotland, having just won six consecutive Carlisle and District League titles and four consecutive League Cups, was admitted to the new division alongside ten others, all from the North East or North Yorkshire. At the end of the season, finishing in second place behind Peterlee Newtown, Gretna were promoted to Division One, where they remained until 1992.

By virtue of joining the Northern League Division One in 1983, Gretna were admitted to the qualifying rounds of the FA Cup. The team's first ever FA Cup game took place on 3 September 1983 with a 3-1 victory over Consett. Playing at right-back that day was a young man from the village with the name of Stuart Rome.

Off the field, the club was beginning to grow too. Around £100,000 was spent upgrading Raydale prior to joining the Northern League, including the purchase of floodlights and the building of a new stand and changing rooms. In 1984 the club adopted a new constitution which laid out its main objective as 'fostering and developing the game of football in the Gretna area'. This document also stated that, in the event of the club being disbanded, all funds and assets would be left in the name of the club for a period of at least ten years after which they would be distributed to sporting or charitable organisations in Gretna – assuming any assets were left.

*

At around 7pm on the evening of 21 December 1988, in their house at Lochmaben just north of the border, Helen MacGregor was showing her husband Ron the Christmas tree which she had newly decorated. Behind the tree, the window suddenly glowed orange. An aircraft known as *Clipper Maid of the Seas*, Pan Am flight 103, crashed on the town of Lockerbie, four miles to the east. Helen, a radiographer at Dumfries Infirmary, immediately realised the potential consequences – although not the cause, the MacGregors initially thought it must have been something to do with the cheese factory just up the road – and telephoned her boss to alert her. The plane, which had set off from London's Heathrow Airport on an intended journey to New York just half an hour earlier, was the victim of a bomb hidden in luggage. The wounded aircraft fell onto the houses in Lockerbie's Sherwood Crescent. 270 people were killed – all of those on board, as well as eleven residents from the town.

As the world struggled to comprehend this awful act of terrorism, the people of south-east Scotland joined others around the world in displaying defiance and kindness. A benefit fund was set up and events were organised to contribute towards it. Two of these events were charity football matches. On 1 March 1989 in Dumfries, Queen of the South hosted a team from Manchester United, brought up by Alex Ferguson. Before that, on 10 January, the smaller village team from Gretna defeated Glasgow Rangers 2-1 in front of a crowd of 2,000. Helen, who had helped to x-ray the bodies from the wreckage, went to the benefit game at Raydale with Ron. It was one of many the couple had started to attend. Soon they began to help out with running the club.

Meanwhile, the quality of football continued to improve and Gretna became the first Scottish team in over 100 years (after Glasgow Rangers in 1887) to reach the first round proper of the FA Cup in November 1990, losing 3-1 to Rochdale after initially holding the English League side to a goalless draw at Raydale.

Having finished third in the Northern League in the 1988-89 season, Gretna went one place better the following year, then won it in 1990-91. However, as the Northern League did not join the pyramid system until the next season, Gretna's prize did not include promotion. Fortunately the team repeated its success and the

Scots were promoted as champions to Northern Premier League Division One in time for the 1992-93 season.

Their first season in the Northern Premier went well, finishing in sixth place, and the following year saw a second – ultimately last – appearance in the FA Cup first round proper. This time the team from the border was defeated 3-2 by Bolton Wanderers in a 'home' match which was actually played in Bolton, following police advice, in November 1993.

But it became apparent that the club's ambitions were not for English success, but to return to Scotland as a proper league side. Ron MacGregor was asked by the chairman, Ian Dalgleish, to use his experience gained in a career in health service management to help prepare a bid when the opportunity arose. That chance came around in 1993 when the Scottish Football League offered membership to two new clubs. Ron and Gretna sent an application, only to lose out to two Highland League teams, Ross County and Inverness Caledonian Thistle. The club's manager, Mike McCartney, who had joined Gretna as a player in 1987 then moved to player-manager a year later, worked to bring Raydale up to scratch for the application, spending the summer labouring in the stands or on the roof, painting and decorating.

McCartney, who had played for clubs as geographically diverse as Southampton and Carlisle United, had not been in favour of the step up to the Northern Premier League. The extra travelling involved had a detrimental effect on Gretna's finances and the club nearly went under in February 1999. In an eerie forerunner of future events, the club was not able to pay the players' wages and Ron MacGregor came to the rescue, paying from his own pocket until the end of the season.

A second application to join the Scottish League was made in 1999, following the Scottish Premier League's decision to expand from ten to twelve clubs. Ron Mac-Gregor had learned from experience and decided to put together an application pack to present to the League members. Despite a much improved bid, Gretna narrowly lost out to two more teams from the north: Elgin City and Peterhead.

In the face of financial concerns, the club continued to grow and a set of objectives to cover the period 1996 to 2000 had been agreed by the committee. The force behind this was the MacGregor partnership, who were keen to introduce a more professional attitude to the club and to maintain and 'if possible, improve' relations with the social club. The latter's membership was split equally with six members representing Gretna FC sitting alongside six separate social club members on the com-mittee. The ambivalent attitude from some of the social club members towards the football club – even to the extent of complaining to visiting teams about the way the latter was run – meant that there was a certain amount of disharmony. The football club, however, pressed on with plans to move forward, aiming to provide 'good quality services' to paying spectators alongside the long-term development of Raydale. Plans for more secure finances (including increasing sponsorship and developing the Sunday market) were put together.

Having been rejected a second time by the Scottish League, for the 1999-00 season the club committed to cost-cutting measures, reducing the wage bill and sacking Assistant Manager George Norrie. By the turn of the year 2000, McCartney was also gone. Years later the ex-manager, who took Gretna to tribunal after being given the push, noted that the financial situation had impacted on his ability to field a team of decent players, complaining that his small squad of fourteen lacked experience: 'We were in the relegation zone by Christmas. I saw the sack coming – managers always do when they are not getting results.'

The next manager, Paddy Lowery, helped the club to avoid relegation but, struggling the next season, by November 2000 he was also gone, replaced by a man called Rowan Alexander.

Alexander had been born in the coastal resort of Ayr but had moved south and been a junior player at Annan Athletic. In 1978, at the age of seventeen, he joined Queen of the South and remained there for five years as they moved from the Scottish Third Division to the Second in 1981. Held in high regard as a player and prolific striker – scoring a goal on average every other game – and following spells at St Mirren, Brentford and Morton, he returned to the Dumfries club in 1995 and became player-manager the following year. The club was struggling in the league, but Alexander took Queens to mid-table by the end of the season. The following year they were challenging for promotion and were beaten in the final of the Challenge Cup by First Division Falkirk.

However, football is a risky business with impatient supporters and owners and as results started to slide, Alexander's position became less secure. Unfortunately for him, this coincided with a time when his private life was coming under intense scrutiny. On New Year's Day 1999, Alexander and his wife separated. Allegedly his career was the cause, or as *The Sun* put it: 'Wife: It's football or me. Boss: I'll sleep at the ground.'

Indeed, the manager did actually move some of his clothes and possessions into the office while he searched for somewhere else to live, but the press speculation and gossip in Dumfries led the club's owner to believe that he had to walk. Alexander clearly felt very bitter about it and argued that he had, to an extent, been the victim of a stitch-up, having previously refused to resign when asked by the directors. 'I was warned if my family problems ended up in the papers I was finished,' he said afterwards. 'The papers had the story the next day and I was sacked… To me it showed the extremes people are prepared to go to just to get people out of their jobs.'

After a short coaching contract in the United States, Alexander returned to Scotland and began applying for jobs, where he was offered the vacant post at Gretna.

2

The final eight years in the short life of Gretna Football Club witnessed the most remarkable story of a British team in recent times. When Rowan Alexander joined in November 2000, the club was struggling, both financially and on the pitch. The sixth-place finish in their first season in Northern Premier Division One (in 1992-93) turned out to be their highest. It became tenth in 1993-94, eleventh in 1994-95, twelfth in 1995-96, sixteenth in 1996-97 and fifteenth in 1997-98. McCartney managed a marginal and brief recovery to twelfth in 1998-99, but was sacked halfway through the next season. Gretna just avoided relegation under Paddy Lowery, finishing nine-teenth out of twenty-two in 1999-00.

Alexander's arrival sparked no immediate revival. When he joined, Gretna had won only five of their fifteen league games, drawing three, and stood with eighteen points out of a possible forty-five – a success rate of 40%. By the end of the season, Gretna climbed to sixteenth in the table with 48 points from 126, a success rate of 38%. If anything, the team's results were actually slightly worse under Alexander, with only a further seven wins. His first game in charge saw a 7-0 away defeat at Matlock Town. Football managers rarely get much time to prove themselves, but at Gretna, Alexander was left in peace right through a fairly bad start to the 2001-02 season (three points after the first eight games, a success rate of 13%). After that, Gretna's march to success really began in earnest.

Alexander was much more than a coach. He had started to instil some professionalism into the way the club was being run. Being faced with what he described as a 'shambles' on his arrival, where only six players turned up for training, Alexander led by example, becoming the groundsman and general manager as well as guiding the players and choosing the team.

The players' annual wage bill was £30,000 and this, along with other expenditure, was financed largely by income from the busy Sunday market which could make over £8,000 some months. The social club also contrib-uted over £1,000 each month. Gate receipts, on the other hand, were fairly negligible. Only sixty-four spectators turned up at Raydale to watch another defeat to Matlock Town on 8 September 2001, although crowds were usually twice that number.

The club's finances seemed stable, but Alexander and others were aware of the higher costs of playing in England and a view had been formed to apply again to the Scottish League at the next available opportunity. The club's eagerness resulted in criticism when Morton FC sacked its staff of fifty due to financial problems at the end of the 2000-01 season. With the club from Greenock granted one month to convince the Scottish Football League that it would be able to fulfil its 2001-02 season fixtures, Gretna's secretary Ian Armour was quoted in the press arguing that there did not need to be any further debate about who should take Morton's place if the Scottish League was not provided with the guarantee. 'We are demanding that Gretna be allowed into the SFL as we were a clear third in the application process behind Peterhead and Elgin City [in 1999],' stated Armour, hastily adding, 'Gretna don't want to appear like vultures but we have got to look after our own situation.'

Morton survived but another chance for Gretna would come soon enough, courtesy of the financial problems being experienced by a couple of other teams around a hundred miles to the north. The first of these was Clyde-bank, who had played in the town of the same name in West Dunbartonshire since 1965, joining the Scottish League one year later. The owners of the club since its inception, the Steedman Brothers, decided in 1996 to sell the football ground, New Kilbowie, promising to build a new 8,000-seater stadium in the town. However when the local council refused planning permission, the club was effectively sentenced to a slow and painful death. Home matches were played first at Greenock Morton's ground (seventeen miles away) and then at Dumbarton (eight miles) but by the spring of 2002, the club was desperately looking for another buyer who might inject some more money.

Meanwhile, over in Lanarkshire, the town of Airdrie was experiencing similar troubles. Airdrieonians were an old club, having been founded, initially as Excelsior FC, in 1878. In 1994 the club sold its ground, Broomfield Park, to the Safeway supermarket chain, promising (like Clydebank) to use the funds to build a new 10,000-seater stadium. The size was deliberate: this was one of the essential criteria which allowed Scottish Premier League admission, although it was later revised down to 6,000. This time the problem was not in gaining planning permission, it was about building according to that permission. The club had promised three football parks, a pavilion and parking for 1,217 cars and seventy coaches. Due to financial constraints the new completed stadium did not contain these as per the original specification, leading to legal action and the entire team bizarrely being sentenced to community service in March of 2002. This was, considering the circumstances, better for the club than a fine.

Airdrieonians' new ground, known as the Shyberry Excelsior, was opened in time for the 1998-99 season, with the club having played home games at Clyde's Cumbernauld stadium, some seven miles to the north, for the intervening four years. Again, there had been financial consequences which had contributed to the club's breach of planning agreements. They never recovered and at the end of the 2001-02 season, on 1 May, Airdrieonians were liquidated, owing some £2.5 million.

This meant that there was a place going in the Scottish Football League and Gretna, along with six other clubs, swung into action. Each club put together its package and on 18 June 2002, seven presentations were made to the twenty-seven chairmen of the Scottish Football League clubs at Glasgow's Hampden Park. From the start of the six-week campaign, Gretna had been one of the favourites along with Gala Fairydean and an as-yet non-existent club that had never actually kicked a ball known as Airdrie United. The other clubs were Cove Rangers and Huntly from the Highland League, and Edinburgh City and Preston Athletic from the East of Scotland League.

The new Airdrie club had been put together following Airdrieonians' extinction by local businessman Jim Ballantyne. Ballantyne had previously headed one of three groups that had looked into buying out Airdrieonians in the last few months of that club's existence but, while others had urged the three to work together and pool resources, none of the groups was able to take over the club and try to resolve the problem of a £2.5 million debt. Of this, £1 million was owed to the local council – North Lanarkshire – and £450,000 was being chased by the construction company which had built the new Excelsior stadium. That company was headed by Bill Barr, who was also the chairman of Ayr United. When Airdrieonians visited Ayr for the last game of the season on 27 April, a pitch invasion by the travelling Lanarkshire support ended with a broken crossbar and an abandoned game. Airdrieonians were not even allowed the dignity of finishing their last ever match.

Within days of the club's demise, it was reported that Ballantyne had registered two new companies, Airdrie FC Ltd and Airdrie Football Club Ltd. He let it be known that a new club would be a separate entity from the old one (and hence nothing to do with the old debts) and that it would be applying for the vacancy in the league. A ground-share arrangement with nearby Albion Rovers was agreed, although it soon became clear that North Lanarkshire Council (which owned the land housing the Excelsior Stadium) would support the new club in renting the stadium from the liquidators. Placing to one side the then purely theoretical issue about old debts in favour of local politics, the council supported Ballantyne's application to the Scottish Football League. When Ballantyne said he had set aside £500,000 for the 'football debts' (money owed to other clubs and players) of the old club – a liability which he had no legal requirement to meet – Scotland's newest club became favourites to win the Scottish League place, which would of course be decided by the other clubs, many of whom would benefit from Ballantyne's guarantee about footballing debts.

However, impressed by the presentation from Gretna, and possibly wary of the precedent it might set for other clubs to disband, walk away from debt and then reform, the thirteen club chairmen in the meeting at Hampden Park voted for the border outfit, compared with eight for Airdrie. It was agonisingly just one short of a majority and a second ballot was called.

Everyone had expected Airdrie to win. The question of whether Gretna were big enough and financially secure enough had arisen before, but this time Ron MacGregor was able to show that, although money was tight, it was sound. Gretna received sixteen votes in the next round. After an absence of fifty-five years, Gretna football was back in Scotland.

The backers of Airdrie United were furious. Journalist Jim Traynor wrote in his *Daily Record* column, 'Yesterday, Scottish football refused to reach out and offer the desperate club a saving hand. Instead, sixteen Scottish League clubs voted to give a berth in our professional setup to a club from the English Unibond League. Please, someone explain that to me before I explode with this rage I have inside.'

That rage went on to compare the great strides being made in football by countries like South Korea (who had that day defeated Italy in the World Cup) with Scotland, which apparently 'continued to implode'. Perhaps more embarrassing was Traynor's wish that the 'sixteen' (whom he seemed to see as some sort of traitors to Scotland) would 'one day soon face extinction' and that 'no one should lift a finger to help these imbeciles who abused their right to vote'.

To be fair, Traynor, a long-standing Airdrie fan, was clearly rather emotionally drained by the episode and in later years he seems to have come round to Gretna, even defending them where others wanted to stick the knife in.

Once the anger subsided, those behind Airdrie United ignored the temptation to admit defeat and, while accepting that Gretna had won, even offering their grudging congratulations, they turned their minds to other opportunities. Looking around the end-of-season battlefield of Scottish football, there were a number of wounded casualties who could be considered easy prey and who might be taken over by this new Airdrie United. The owners of Hamilton Academicals even tried to call Ballantyne's bluff, assuming that a takeover of that club would mean that it would continue to be based in Hamilton, a potentially more lucrative possibility than Airdrie. Ballantyne had, after all, apparently half a million in the bank and he might be persuaded to invest that in Hamilton. However, Ballantyne was only interested in senior football in Airdrie itself and what he needed was a mortally wounded Scottish League club which he could buy and ship to his town, changing its name and kit on the journey, but keeping its place in the Scottish Football League. Struggling Clydebank seemed like the perfect opportunity.

Clydebank had not had a home ground for six years and were in the hands of the administrator, Bryan Jackson. Having given the United Clydebank Supporters (UCS) group a year to raise £160,000 to buy the club, an approach was made within two days of the Scottish League vote by Ballantyne. Aware of the risky approach he was taking, the Airdrie United chairman-elect then sought, and was given, a guarantee on 1 July by the SFL Management Committee that such a takeover would be allowed. Perhaps surprised or cowed by the reaction to the 18 June vote, SFL Secretary Peter Donald noted his regret that the name of Clydebank would not continue, but stated, 'Currently the opportunities that are available in Airdrie – the custom-built new stadium – meant that we thought in the longer term, this would be more beneficial to the League and its member clubs.'

The takeover was held up for a few more days with the administrator allowing UCS one last chance to raise the money, but the outcome was inevitable and Airdrie United took Clydebank's place in the league, in the end going one better than Gretna, as Clydebank had been in the higher Second Division. Outrage was then directed at, rather than from, Airdrie United. To all intents and purposes the new club was a straight replacement but without having to pay off the debt. By managing to kill off another club in the process, the new one ensured league status continued in the town.

Meanwhile, preparations down in Gretna had been frantic. 'There was a fearsome checklist,' recalls Ron Mac-

Gregor. 'We had to remove the gravel from the terraces, level the pitch. It was endless and because the contractors knew we had a tight deadline, we didn't exactly get the best deal for any of this work.' These were scenes reminiscent of fifty-five years before when the club had employed the services of prisoners of war to get Raydale fit and ready for the Carlisle and District League, or of thirty-five years later, preparing for the Northern League. This time however, the club was returning home and the excitement in the town was widely reported.

Peter Donald regarded Gretna's homecoming as a shot across the bows of the Old Firm of Rangers and Celtic, who were allegedly looking at the time to leave Scotland and join the much more lucrative English Football League system. He also praised Gretna's improvements, both at Raydale and in the bid since the previous applications. The village registrar Sheila Wallace said, in what at the time could possibly have been taken as exaggeration (but later – at least for a while – proved true), 'We've always been famous for weddings, now we're going to be known for football as well … it will give the area some added status.' In the same newspaper, the vote was seen as one part of a day of victory for the underdogs, quoting South Korea's victory of Italy in quite a different way from its use by Jim Traynor. Meanwhile the *Mirror* that same day reminded its readers that football finances were precarious 'with so many Scottish clubs teetering on the brink of bankruptcy'.

For now, such issues were at the back of Gretna minds. The work at Raydale continued and everything was complete for Gretna's first pre-season friendly as a Scottish League team on 13 July against Falkirk – all apart from one forgivable and forgotten detail. Those attending the game possibly enjoyed the patriotic touch of having Lions Rampant for the corner flags, but will not have known that such livery was a hasty purchase from the nearby Gretna Gateway Outlet Village when someone belatedly realised that the old flags still had English Unibond League logos on them.

Gretna played well, holding Falkirk until Owen Coyle scored late in the game. This was the same Owen Coyle who had scored two late goals against Gretna for Bolton in the FA Cup in 1993. The same Owen Coyle who had been sentenced along with the rest of the Airdrieonians team for community service earlier that year. The same Owen Coyle who Gretna would eventually get one over by scoring a far more spectacular and more important late goal to pip his team to a far bigger prize.

3

When Rowan Alexander joined Gretna in 2000, he made it clear his goal was to play in the Scottish League. However, hand-in-hand with that ambition was a desire to put the club on a more robust and developmental basis. With a budget of around £800 per week, £100 of which was his meagre salary, Alexander realised that investment in youth was necessary; a cheaper, but perhaps more successful, way of growing players for the club. A flat was purchased for £3,000 to house young players on the club's Skillseekers course. This was a Scottish government initiative aimed at young people aged between sixteen and nineteen who were not at school or college. The programme was designed to help the youngsters develop skills and become better equipped for the world of work.

Alexander was still mowing the grass and doing a spot of painting and decorating where required while getting his team ready for their first game in the league, knowing the eyes of the world would be watching. Indeed an amazing crowd of around 1,800 – not much less than the total number of residents in the village – turned up for the opener against Greenock Morton on Saturday 3 August. The match was not without significance for the Gretna manager. During his nine seasons at Greenock between 1986 and 1995, Alexander had been a Morton favourite, scoring 98 goals in 310 games.

During the summer, Alexander had brought some experience into the squad by persuading Davie Irons, the player-manager of Annan, to join. Irons, who had celebrated his forty-first birthday in July 2002, was only six months younger than Alexander and the two of them carried the tags of being the oldest players in the Scottish League.

Gretna needed only nineteen seconds to make their mark on Scottish football. Matthew Henney took advantage of a poor clearance from the Morton goalkeeper and scored the first goal of the 2002-03 league season. Sadly, Gretna were unable to hold onto their lead and the match (in which Alexander had come on as a second-half sub) ended 1-1. Nevertheless it was a good result against the team who were favourites to win the division, having survived their financial difficulties of recent years.

In 2002-03, the Scottish Third Division had ten teams (it still does in 2015, although is now known as League Two) with everyone playing each other four times: twice at home, twice away. Gretna had moved on from playing the likes of Spennymoor United, Workington and Harrogate Town and would now face journeys to the far north (Peterhead and Elgin), Tayside and Fife (Montrose and East Fife) and the central belt (Greenock Morton, Coatbridge's Albion Rovers, Stirling Albion, East Stirlingshire – who play in Falkirk, not Stirling – and Queen's Park).

Queen's Park is the oldest football club in Scotland, having been founded in 1867. They are also still a purely amateur team, 'playing' according to their motto, simply 'for the sake of playing' (*ludere causa ludendi*). They also, rather eerily, host their home games at Scotland's national stadium, the 52,000-capacity all-seater Hampden Park. It was here that Gretna travelled to for their second game, where they lost 2-1 to Queen's Park in the Scottish Challenge Cup, with Mark Dobie scoring Gretna's goal. The defeat appears to have galvanised the club as Gretna then won their next three league games and found themselves as league leaders, albeit briefly. Following defeats by Queen's Park, Peterhead, Stirling Albion and East Fife, Gretna had settled in sixth place by mid-October and remained there for the rest of the season. Morton eventually won the division, with East Fife also promoted.

As far as cup competitions went, as well as the defeat by Queen's Park in the Challenge Cup (which was open to all teams in the Scottish Football League, but not the

Premier League), Gretna also fell at the first hurdle in the League Cup, losing 2-1 at home to East Fife. The club did manage to get to the third round of the Scottish Cup (after beating Cove Rangers 3-0) where they lost 2-1 after a good effort against First Division Clyde.

At the end of the season, the verdict was that the new entrants had done themselves proud. They had finished sixth in the division, but twelve points above seventh-place Montrose and thirty-two points above East Stirlingshire, who were shortly to became infamous as 'the worst team in Britain', finishing bottom of the league for the next four seasons as well. In 2003-04 they would gather only eight points. Gretna had established themselves on the pitch while home attendances ended up averaging 418 – much higher than had been anticipated by anyone at the start of the season.

Off the pitch, however, something even more significant had been quietly taking place during the club's first season in Scottish football.

The Pennywell housing scheme in Sunderland was built after the Second World War and has over the years gained a reputation for being one of the toughest areas in the North East. It is here that Brooks Mileson was born on 13 November 1947, exactly two months after fledgling Gretna FC had played their first ever game at the new Raydale Park. Mileson's story – echoed later by that of some of the teams he supported financially – was a classic rags-to-riches tale, the determined hero fighting against all the odds. He had a deeply religious upbringing amidst poverty – his parents and their five children lived in a two-bedroom house on the estate – and his Christian nature no doubt underpinned the side of his character which led him to throw his money, whatever the consequences, at those he thought deserved it. His obstinacy – later exemplified in a refusal to hobnob in the boardrooms of the richer clubs – is most famously seen in the reaction to a horrific accident the eleven-year-old Brooks suffered, when a wall of sand fell on him while playing in a quarry with six of his mates.

The accident broke his back, dislocated his hips and caused further injuries to his kidney, which later had to be removed, and right leg. Told he would never walk again, Mileson decided otherwise and would wait until his parents were asleep before getting out of bed and pulling himself around the furniture, determined to prove everyone wrong. Then the doctors told him he would not be able to take part in sport. 'To me,' he would later recall, 'it was like they were saying, OK smart-arse, you can walk, but you won't be able to run.' Of course he eventually did, representing England in 1967 in the World Junior Cross-Country Championships. He won the bronze medal.

Mileson had a similarly successful approach to business. Leaving school at the age of sixteen, he studied and qualified as an accountant. When, as a victim of the economic downturn, he was made redundant during the 1980s, he started his own company, a construction firm, and later moved into insurance and car hire. This brought him wealth and during the 1990s he started to hand out his money to various sporting causes – principally football.

By 1992 he was sponsoring Whitby Town FC, becoming their president three years later. In 1998, the Albany Group which he had founded began a ten-year sponsorship of the Northern League (the one Gretna had entered in 1982), eventually pumping some half a million pounds into it. Mileson had moved over the Pennines by then and was living just outside Carlisle, ten miles south of Gretna and the border, and had become a fan of that city's team. At that stage his wealth was substantial but it would greatly increase when he sold the Albany Group (in which he had an 80% stake) in 2004 for a reputed £46.8 million and other companies for something over £20 million.

In 1999, Mileson made an approach to the owner of Carlisle United, Michael Knighton, who had declared that he was looking to sell up. Knighton was perhaps an even more colourful character. Another self-made businessman, he had nearly bought Manchester United for £20 million in 1989 – a deal which would have proved to be one of the century's cleverest, given that twenty-five years later the club is valued at over £2 billion. However the deal fell through when Knighton's partners pulled out, although not before he had appeared on the pitch at Old Trafford and scored an imaginary hat-trick into an empty net before the opening Premier League game of the 1989-90 season. As part recompense, Knighton was given a place on the Board of Directors, a position he retained until 1992 when he purchased Carlisle United, promising

Premiership status by the end of the decade. Despite some early successes at Carlisle, Knighton's relationship with the fans from the border city worsened dramatically following a series of rather curious events. Rightly or wrongly, there was a perception that Knighton was not investing enough in the team. To be fair, a brand new stand was built during his time there, although it did overreach the ground by approximately twenty metres. Away fans who sit too near the end are still unable to see the game properly and instead find themselves gazing down on the terraces behind one of the goals. This had been done deliberately; Knighton's plan was to move the pitch so that land behind the stadium could be used for a hotel, golf course, a lake for watersports and a wildlife reserve. None of this was ever built and Knighton's reputation suffered further when, in 1997, he sacked manager Mervyn Day and – it is said – appointed himself manager, something he has always denied, insisting that he was just a 'front' for his coaches. His family were employed at the club (his son was a registered player) and then in 1999 he sold the club's only goalkeeper, Tony Caig (who would later play for Gretna), and had to rely on a special dispensation from the Football League to bring a player on loan to stand between the posts. That on-loan goalkeeper, Jimmy Glass, scored an injury-time winner against Plymouth on the last day of the season to keep Carlisle United in the Football League.

Around the time that Jimmy was being Roy of the Rovers, Mileson and Knighton were discussing a possible sale of the club, but by December 1999 it was clear that their respective valuations were miles apart. In hindsight, Mileson was almost too desperate to become Carlisle's owner and some have wondered how much leverage – and later satisfaction – that presented to Knighton.

In September 2000, Knighton and his wife were banned from being company directors following a Department for Trade and Industry investigation into one of their businesses, St David's School in Huddersfield, where Michael had been a teacher, then headmaster. The private school had gone bust in 1995, just around the time Knighton claimed that he had seen a UFO hovering close to the school. However, he still owned 93% of Carlisle United and once again apparently set out to find a buyer. In January 2001, it was announced that he had been successful and that 60% of the club was being sold to Mamcarr – an unidentified group, based in Gibraltar – and another 25% to Borders-based millionaire Stephen Brown.

Farcically, Stephen Brown was in fact no millionaire, but an ex-curry house waiter living in sheltered housing in Peebles. His experience of football management appears to have been restricted to three months with non-league Gala Fairydean, although that hadn't even gone well. As for Mamcarr? Conspiracy theorists pointed out that the name was made up of the initials of Michael Knighton's family: Michael, Albert (father), Mark (son), Chevonne Anna (daughter), Rosemary (wife), Rory (son).

In time that did not matter. The proposed sale simply appears to have come to a halt, if indeed it had ever started. Knighton instead declared that other interested parties were involved, and again one of these was Brooks Mileson. In August 2001, the local paper was reporting that Mileson was within days of taking over, but again the deal fell through with accusation and counter-accusation as to whether the real millionaire from Sunderland had sufficient funds. Knighton finally sold the club to Irishman John Courtney (initially Courtney and Mileson had been working on a joint bid) in July 2002.

During these years, Mileson had briefly been the owner of Scarborough FC. The club on the North Yorkshire coast had faced financial difficulties and, in August 2000, Mileson had stepped in to take over until a permanent buyer could be found. In the process he had ploughed, according to some sources, more than £750,000 of his own money into the club. Mileson sold Scarborough (making no profit) after eight months, although the financial issues never really went away and the club went into liquidation in 2007, before being re-founded.

On 3 August 2002, one week after his final attempt to purchase Carlisle United had come to nothing, Mileson attended Raydale for the first time as part of a Northern League delegation at Gretna's inaugural Scottish Football League game against Morton. Despite living less than ten miles away, Mileson had never visited Gretna's home ground, but very quickly he started to become involved. Rowan Alexander left a positive impression on Mileson and the millionaire agreed to sponsor the club's Skillseek-ers programme after another firm had pulled out. This would be the first £20,000 of around £8 million which he would spend on the club over the next five years.

By now, it had become apparent to all who met him that Mileson was not exactly a picture of health. As well as his childhood traumas, he suffered from ME and allegedly lived on a diet of cigarettes and Lucozade. Having avoid-ing tobacco until he was forty-eight, Mileson seemed to be making up for lost time, making his way through four or five packets every day. 'Jesus Christ, who the hell is this?' thought Alexander when he was approached by Mileson with that first cheque. The answer will probably never be fully known, but we can certainly think of a mixture of shrewd business acumen mixed with reckless abandon regarding his money and a desire simply to have some fun. All of this was underpinned by a deep-seated belief to help his fellow man.

Mileson also knew a footballing opportunity when he saw one. He came back to Raydale a second and third time, and eventually became a fan of the club. 'He didn't sweep into the boardroom or anything like that,' recalls Ron MacGregor, but when the committee began to ask for his advice, Mileson freely gave it. When the request to join formally was eventually made, Mileson told the club that they needed to think of becoming a limited company and that he would help out although he didn't, according to MacGregor, want to 'control the club or be announced as the new owner'.

However, by January 2003, the club's committee had taken the decision to work 'in parallel' with 'Brooks Mileson's advisors' and to review a number of areas. These included a decision to move to limited company status, the issuing of shares, the appointment of directors, company secretary and chief executive, team management and budget, youth development, the upgrading of ground to comply with Scottish Football League requirements, income generation and sponsorship, financial reporting and proper contracts of employment.

The last of these was to include the team manager/groundsman issue – Rowan Alexander was still carrying out both roles. Mileson, now clearly in charge despite denials to the contrary, walked up to Alexander and asked him which job he wanted – he couldn't have both. Alexander had no hesitation in confirming that it would be the manager's post.

Financially, Gretna had been finding things tight, and were struggling to pay off the £50,000 that had been quickly invested the previous summer to bring Raydale up to scratch for Scottish League requirements. In that first season, projected turnover was around a quarter of a million pounds. Gate receipts on the opening day were £10,000, but that was a one-off with around 1,800 in attendance; crowd averages dropped to 418. That was still, it should be noted, three times higher than when the team had been competing in the English league. TV money was a welcome novelty, adding a few thousand pounds to the accounts, but the club continued to rely heavily on the Sunday market, which brought in £40,000 every year.

Mileson had donated £20,000 to the club's Skillseekers programme and now he wiped out their £50,000 debt at one stroke. 'I looked upon it as the club having a clean sheet,' he said later. 'They were a part-time club going nowhere because of lack of finance from a small town.' At the same time he was insistent that the club placed itself on a more professional footing. He would provide the cash, but the board of directors would have to do their bit, and this is what led to the club seminar on 19 January 2003 where it was agreed to take the club forward.

During the spring of 2003, despite rumours linking Mileson with a takeover of York City FC, certain legal moves were made which tightened Mileson's grip on Gretna. On 14 May the innocently named 48 Shelf (112) Ltd was formed with an initial share capital of 1,000 £1 shares. Within two weeks it became Gretna Football Club Ltd with Helen MacGregor as company secretary and other directors, including Mileson's long-standing business colleague Keith Agar. Mileson himself did not become a director at first, but by the beginning of June, the BBC was reporting that he was now the majority shareholder and would introduce a new board at Raydale Park. Agar became managing director, Ron MacGregor moved from club secretary to chairman, and the outgoing chairman, Brian Fulton, was awarded the title of president. The initial intention was to offer supporters shares in the club in batches of 100 and these were approved for the following: Helen MacGregor, Ron MacGregor, Brian Fulton, John Smith, Alan Watson, Steven Barker (the club's commercial manager), Rowan Alexander, William Hume, Alan Dalrymple, Jack Gass, Ian Dalgleish and Derek Frye. Collectively these shares were dwarfed by the 54,600 owned by Mileson through his company, Heartshape.

Keith Agar's job as managing director lasted only one month with Mileson, who himself finally joined the board in July, declaring that the club did not need a full-time MD, taking on the role himself. Now financially secure, Gretna prepared for their second season in the Scottish League.

4

Expenditure and expectations rocketed. Rowan Alexander publicly waved goodbye to the old days by declaring that although the club had stood by the players who had been with the team in the Unibond League for the first season in Scotland, Gretna now had to 'kick on'. Those in the squad who remained were largely given full-time contracts but they were soon joined by an array of new talent unheard of for a mid-table Third Division club.

The first indication that something was going on was the rumour that a set of twins from England would be joining. Dean Holdsworth was a striker who had just helped Rushden and Diamonds win the English Division

Three title. His brother, David, was a defender at Scarborough. Now aged thirty-four, both had played for much bigger teams during their career. Five years previously Dean had been sold to Bolton from Wimbledon for £3.5 million and he had also played for Watford, Coventry and Swansea. David had also played for Bolton and Watford, as well as Sheffield United and Birmingham City (whom he cost £1.25 million). Both had appeared for England: David at under-21 level, Dean at 'B' level. Although the brothers were in the twilight of their career, the move signalled Gretna's ambition. In the end only David actually arrived at Raydale; his brother chose instead to return to Wimbledon, who were playing in the second tier and had just entered administration ahead of their imminent move to Milton Keynes.

Ambition was further expressed by Gretna's capture of Martin Cameron, a striker from Scottish First Division St Mirren, and of midfielder Danny Lennon, who was playing in the Scottish Premier League with Partick Thistle. These signings provoked more than a flicker of interest on some of the internet football forums. 'Football is going mad but someone has money to burn. Clearly Gretna will be promotion favourites,' posted one disgruntled St Mirren fan. 'I nearly fell on the ground... they have a minted new owner,' wrote another.

By the time the season kicked off, Gretna had added Paul O'Neill (from Macclesfield), James Allen (Queens Park), Gary Cohen (Scarborough), Richard Robb (on loan from St Mirren) and Richard Prokas, ex-Carlisle

United, Cambridge United and Workington Reds, to their bulging squad. Then, and more significantly as it would turn out, a sortie over the border brought Mark Birch, Ryan Baldacchino and Lee Madison from Carlisle and the ex-Carlisle striker, Ian Stevens, from Barrow. There were even rumours at the beginning of August, played down by Alexander, of a potential bid for ex-Scotland international Colin Hendry.

Belief was strong and hardly diminished when Gretna won the pre-season Brewers Cup, a four-team tournament played in Annan. The other participants were Annan Athletic, Stranraer and Livingston. The team from the border beat Premier League Livingston 3-1 in the final, a game notable for the red card shown to the Premier League's side's goalkeeper, Alan Main.

The first competitive match of the season was therefore a bit of an anti-climax: Gretna lost 5-0 at home to First Division side (and eventual winners of that division) Inverness Caledonian Thistle in the Challenge Cup. Nevertheless the optimism at the club continued with architects commissioned to look at building a new stadium at Raydale, funded of course by Mileson, who had become less shy about displaying his wealth. He now spoke openly to the press about paying off the club's debt and of the fact that the annual wage bill would now exceed half a million pounds. The money came with conditions, however: 'I gave Rowan a budget and I demand success – it is a requirement.'

These days most football fans both dream and are wary of the prospect of a rich benefactor arriving at their club with a chequebook in one hand and a wish list in the other. The changes at their club had caused a ripple of disquiet in Gretna – a ripple which would be much exaggerated in later years – and before the start of the season, Mileson sought to quell any unrest by meeting with Dumfries MP Russell Brown and a group of local residents. Mileson emphasised that he wanted to see the community become part of the club – hence the offer of selling shares to supporters – and he was backed by the MP who claimed the anxiety had been caused by ridiculous rumours and scaremongering. The meeting, he added, led to people feeling much more relaxed. To illustrate his commitment to the club's grassroots, Mileson then invited Mark Hampson on to the board as a non-executive director. Mark was chairman of the Gretna Supporters' Club which in turn received a donation from Mileson to help with travel expenses.

With this background, Gretna's start to the league campaign was surprising and disappointing. By early October, the only full-time professional club in the Third Division supposedly filled with higher quality than their rivals, had won just two of their first eight league games, drawing four others. Ten points from a potential twenty-four left Gretna twelve behind league leaders Stirling Albion. At the start of the season, Assistant Manager Derek Frye had predicted success. 'There's no reason why we should under-achieve,' he said, looking forward to the championship trophy being presented at Hampden where Gretna were due to play Queens Park on the last day of the season the following May. These words came back to haunt Frye when Rowan Alexander took the decision to sack him on 8 October along with head coach Toby Patterson. Such action seemed ruthless – a sign of the seriousness of Gretna's intentions perhaps; Frye had helped Alexander develop the Scottish Football League bid. But it seemed to work, with the team winning seven of the next eight games and drawing the other. The improvement lifted Gretna to third in the division, just outside the important top two positions which led to promotion.

During the January transfer window, Alexander made Ryan Baldacchino's loan from Carlisle permanent and also brought in Ryan's former Carlisle colleagues, Brian Wake and Derek Townsley. The latter, a versatile player who could cover almost any position, was a former postman who had played for Gretna in the Northern Premier League. He had scored the opening goal in the 3-2 defeat by Bolton in November 1993 when Gretna had been the last ever Scottish team to play in the proper rounds of the FA Cup. Following spells at Queen of the South, Motherwell and Hibernian, Townsley had been at Oxford United since 1993 but had been released by them at that point struggling in English League One. Townsley, going on thirty-one, had been eagerly sought by Carlisle United's manager, Paul Simpson, who tried to convince him to return to his home town club. However, Carlisle were unable to match Mileson's offer of a three-year contract. 'That swayed it,' said Simpson with some regret.

The squad was balanced by bidding farewell to Jamie McCaig and Keith Knox, who went to Albion Rovers and Stenhousemuir, while Paul O'Neill, a summer signing from Macclesfield, went on loan to Scarborough. Although Gretna's performance improved very marginally after the New Year, it was not enough to win the much sought-after promotion, and Gretna remained in third place until the end of the season. Defeat at Stranraer on 1 May meant that Stranraer and Stirling Albion stepped up to the Second Division. Gretna's Scottish Cup dreams ended at the third round stage with a 2-0 defeat at First Division Clyde in January. The close of the season had not been helped by an injury to top-scorer Martin Cameron at the end of March.

Failure to gain promotion had not been cheap. The club's first submitted set of accounts since becoming a limited company – for the period ending 31 May 2004 – showed that Mileson had pumped in over £741,000 of his own cash. A wage bill of more than half a million pounds was unsustainable at this level and Gretna still made a loss of £345,000 for the year.

However, for the moment at least, it seemed that money was no object. Mileson's wealth was about to grow further still with the forthcoming sale of the Albany Group, which would eventually cost the buying company, Helphire, more than £46 million. A number of clubs and other sporting associations continued to benefit from his philanthropy. Despite his disappointment two years previous when he had failed to become the owner of Carlisle United, support to his neighbours continued with an agreement to pay the wages of any new signings for the English club 'for the entirety of their contracts' without anything in return. A mutual love-in between Mileson and new Carlisle owner Fred Story was played out in the local press: 'I think for the first time during my support of the club we have a man in Fred who will not give us wild promises or hopes ... His efforts will be directed at solving the huge financial problems at the club and putting Carlisle United on a proper financial and business footing.'

Story returned the good wishes: 'I couldn't believe it when he offered to pay the wages of any new players with nothing in return. I never expected such an act of generosity. This marvellous gesture is one that we will not be abusing.'

The money paid for the wages of two of Carlisle's better players over the next few years, Chris Lumsden and Karl Hawley. Mileson's charity continued with a donation later in the year to the Carlisle United Supporters' Trust of £600,000 – a sum which was to be used by the Trust to purchase a large minority share of the club. Unfortunately this was one step too far for the suspicious board of Carlisle United and was the root of a falling out between the two millionaire football club owners.

Other acts of selflessness can be evidenced. In August, Mileson presented a cheque for £25,000 to young local athlete Jordan Fleary to contribute to his accommodation costs at Loughborough University where he would benefit from the top of the range sporting facilities. Back in the world of football, his sponsorship of the Northern League continued.

Mileson's support for Gretna did not appear to have been diminished by such gestures to other groups, nor indeed by Mileson's passing interest in buying Darlington FC in January of 2004. If anything, his ambitions for the border club deepened. In June he resurrected the idea of a new stadium at Raydale. However, whereas the previous year the plans were for a 4,000-capacity ground which would match their aspirations to reach the First Division, this time around, summer 2004, the vision was for something good enough in the Scottish Premier League. The SPL-compliant stadium would need 6,000 seats following a revision to the rules, although the Gretna owner did at least question the wisdom of such requirements. '6,000 is still twice the size of the village. I've seen examples elsewhere when people have built huge stadiums and regretted it,' he said, possibly referring to the case at Airdrie and almost-case at Clydebank. Nevertheless he remained determined to reach the Scottish Premier League within the next few years. 'If not four, five,' he predicted. 'We're really pushing the boat out this season.'

In saying this, Mileson was referring to the stream of new recruits who had been arriving at Raydale for the second consecutive summer, some of them no doubt tempted by wage deals not usually available at this level.

Leading the way had been Andy Aitken, a 26-year-old defender who had spent the previous eight years at Queen of the South. Aitken was joined by 33-year-old David Bingham who opted to join the Third Division side rather than stay with Inverness Caledonian Thistle, who were moving up to the Scottish Premier League.

When Lee Maddison was tragically diagnosed with cancer in July 2004, Mileson once again showed his caring side by declaring that no matter what state the player returned in, once he was better, the club would find a role for him. As cover on the pitch, 33-year-old Jamie McQuilken was signed from St Johnstone, on a loan deal lasting until Christmas. Next came 35-year-old striker Andy Smith from Clyde and 36-year-old goalkeeper Alan Main. Main had played some eight years for St Johnstone and nine with Dundee United, and even sat on the substitutes' bench of the national team. Before joining Gretna he had been at Livingston, yet another Scottish club facing financial pressures, and had been one of five players asked to take a pay cut earlier in the year. Joining Gretna with a three-year deal gave the goalkeeper some financial stability, although he could not immediately play as he was still recuperating from surgery on his back.

The new signings were not all veterans who would be seeing their days out on a good salary on the border. Next came 24-year-old Kenny Deuchar, a prolific striker who had just scored thirty-five goals in seventy-seven games for East Fife, four of them against Gretna. Deuchar had combined playing part-time for the Fifers with his job as a doctor. His new contract allowed him to reduce his time spent healing the sick, although he was keen to keep his hand in, working one day a week at Wishaw General Hospital near Motherwell. To augment the midfield, Mark Boyd (aged twenty-three) was signed from Carlisle United and Bryan Gilfillan (aged nineteen) arrived from Cowdenbeath. An attempt to prise promising forward Alan Gow, then aged twenty-one, from Airdrie failed.

The new squad benefited from training at a luxury complex in Verona, Italy before following Manchester City to an Outward Bounds course in the Lake District. The *News and Star* in Carlisle highlighted the contrast with Carlisle United's preparations for the new season. 'A colleague,' wrote sports journalist Amanda Little, 'spotted a twenty-something, track-suited lad stepping out of a spanking new, top-of-the-range car at the Sands Centre last weekend, and wondered how a youngster could afford such a vehicle. Then he understood when he saw him meeting up with the rest of the Gretna squad assembling in the foyer for a training session.'

The preparations did not stop with the squad. Raydale Park was given a £60,000 makeover with the pitch being re-laid and extended and a new underground drainage system put in. A retractable players' tunnel was also installed, partly in response to an alleged assault on referee Cammy Melville by a home supporter in the previous season's 1-0 defeat by Cowdenbeath. Gretna could easily afford the £250 fine handed to them, but the new measures would at least prevent such an incident reoccurring. Finally, in a move which provoked a mixed reaction among Gretna's fans, the traditional black and white hooped strip was redesigned, becoming all white except for a black band running down the arms.

With wages now costing more than £750,000 per year, expectations were even higher than they had been the previous year. Mileson brushed aside any talk about Rowan Alexander's position being at risk if the team failed to perform on the pitch and the manager himself promised that success would arrive in the coming season. There was some relief then when the opening competitive match of the season, a home tie in the Challenge Cup against fellow Third Division team Montrose, ended in a 3-0 win, with two of the new veterans, David Bingham and Andy Smith, both grabbing a goal. The league campaign got underway at Raydale on 7 August against Albion Rovers. A respectable crowd of 646 watched the league favourites score six goals with no reply to install themselves at the top of the division.

The *Sunday Herald* had preceded the season with a major article about the ever-growing club. 'At this rate,' journalist Stewart Fisher noted, 'manager Rowan Alexander is likely to have more players than supporters.' The average home league attendance in the previous season had in fact been 465 – not much of an increase on 2002-03's 418 but still some way higher than when the club had been playing in the English system. These sorts of numbers would struggle to bring £70,000 in gate receipts each year. Gretna had no hope of covering the staggering wage bill, which would require home attendances in the 4,000s rather than the 400s, a target that was not possible in cramped Raydale. Nevertheless, that first league attendance was certainly higher than previous crowds, and was a sign of things to come.

The second league game produced a bit of a scare for the Black and Whites. Gretna travelled to Falkirk on 14 August to what ought to have been, at least on paper, a foregone conclusion against East Stirlingshire, the worst team in Britain. Their abysmal record had spurred journalist Jeff Connor into writing a book about the club. In *Pointless: A Season with Britain's Worst Football Team*, Connor unsurprisingly describes the late summer encounter with Gretna as a David v Goliath encounter. The chapter, titled 'Big Time Billys', mentions Gretna's luxury bus depositing a group of 'Fancy Dans' and at least one stunning wife, concentrating on David Bingham and his need to maintain 'a young family and four-wheel-drive vehicle'.

Connor recalls the envy of other clubs – the Gretna players had been promised a winter holiday in sunny La Manga if they were top of the division at Christmas – and his presence in the home dressing room allowed him to record what Gretna fans had imagined would be happening in the build up to many a game. 'They are on mega money and think they are someone,' mocked East Stirlingshire's manager Dennis Newall. 'They are no one. That Bingham, what's he doing playing here? Townsley, they're slumming it and they think you're just here to make up the numbers.

Now when they have the ball, you go right through them. I want their physio to be living on that pitch.'

The pep-talk worked and although Andy Aitken put the visitors ahead after thirty-four minutes, the equaliser came three minutes after that. On forty-one minutes, Derek Townsley demonstrated that he did in fact know what he was doing here and scored what turned out to be the winner. In the latter stages of the second half Gordon Parks came on for The Shire and nearly got on the scoresheet – twice. His first attempt went in the net but was marked offside. His second hit the crossbar in the last minute. Gretna survived and remained at the top of the table with six points from a possible six.

The next few matches saw some mixed results, including losses at Queen's Park (league) and Falkirk (Challenge Cup) and a draw at Peterhead in the league. After this there was no stopping the Black and Whites. The next fourteen games saw fourteen wins, including a 2-1 victory on 13 November over Peterhead in front of an astonishing 2,200 spectators, which put Gretna back again in top spot and marked Alexander's fourth year at the club. In those fourteen games Gretna had also found their striking boots. Sixty goals were scored (twenty-one by Deuchar, fifteen by Bingham) with only twelve conceded. The results included an 8-1 win at home against East Stirlingshire and an 8-0 victory away at Cowdenbeath. Poor Albion Rovers faced Gretna in two of those games and conceded six goals in both. The players had earned their promised winter break in the sun.

The extraordinary run was slowed by a 1-1 draw away to Queen's Park – the only team who had defeated Gretna in the league up to this point – but the players recovered to bounce back immediately by defeating Cowdenbeath, 2-0 this time, in preparation for their Scottish Cup third round game against Premier League side Dundee United.

It was almost certainly Gretna's biggest game to date and it would be a good test for a side which allegedly included players of Premier League standard. To ensure a packed Raydale, whose capacity had been temporarily enhanced by the erection of a steel stand at the Solway end of the ground, Mileson bought all of the tickets and handed them out free to supporters. The generosity was extended to the visitors and a large allocation was sent north in the post to Dundee. Mileson also handed a cheque for £5,000 over to the Arab Trust. The trust took its title from the nickname used for Dundee United which itself allegedly derives from the 1962/63 season when bad weather led the club to attempt to thaw their pitch using a tar-burning trunk. The effort succeeded in burning all the grass. Sand was then poured onto the pitch giving the appearance of a beach, or, perhaps, an Arabian desert.

The game had been due to take place on the 8 January but fell victim to the Scottish winter and was rearranged for the following Tuesday. The United team set off in appalling weather only to reach Gretna and be told that the game, due to start at 7.45, had been shelved just four hours before kick-off. Justifiably angry, the visitors com-plained to the Scottish FA, although their wrath was not directed at Gretna. Rowan Alexander was more sanguine. 'I've played in worse conditions,' he said, knowing that it meant his team would now face three games in seven days.

When it finally took place, the cup game had been turned by Mileson into an entertainment extravaganza, complete with brass bands, clowns and fire-eaters. After nineteen minutes, Gretna were losing 3-0 and the cup adventure was turning into a nightmare. However, the players rallied and goals from Kenny Deuchar and Mark Birch just before and after half-time made things interesting. United eventually won 4-3 but the Third Division leaders had, as they say in the land of footballing clichés, acquitted themselves well. The world was beginning to notice what was going on at Raydale. Within a few days Kenny Deuchar was being interviewed for an article in the national newspaper, the *Independent*, and Bryan Gilfillan was selected for the Northern Ireland Under-21 squad for a game in which he would be watched by his fellow Gretna squad members – all at Mileson's expense of course.

Deuchar had been interviewed at his kitchen table and was asked about his goalscoring. The newspaper presented the evidence which showed that he was actually the most prolific scorer in world football. His twenty goals in fifteen games gave him an average of 1.47 goals each time he put on his boots. This was better than players such as Thierry Henry (Arsenal, 0.7 goals per game), John Hartson (Celtic, 0.73) and Samuel Eto'o (Barcelona, 0.74). The only player to come near him was Tomasz Frankowski who played in Poland for Wisla Krakow (1.46). Also on that list was David Graham at Second Division Stranraer. Graham would be a Gretna player within days.

Kenny Deuchar had already become something of a minor celebrity thanks to the constant references to him as 'the good doctor' from Jeff Stelling on Sky Sports. Deuchar had written to Stelling to thank him, adding that his grandmother, Mae, was the presenter's biggest fan. Inevitably when Kenny's next goal hit the back of the net, Mae was mentioned too. 'My gran was buzzing for days,' smiled Deuchar.

The cup game did take its toll on the Gretna players who travelled the long road to Peterhead the following Saturday and went down to a 4-2 defeat. However, they remained top of the division with fourteen games to go.

In January, Alexander had further bolstered the squad. There were two signings from the Scottish premier League – Steve Tosh, a 31-year-old midfielder who had still been part of Aberdeen's first team, and Chris Innes, twenty-eight, a defender from Dundee United. Further experience came with Davie Nicholls (aged thirty-two) from First Division leaders Falkirk and 35-year-old old Derek Collins who joined from Morton.

In terms of youth, the aforementioned prolific goal-scorer David Graham arrived, aged twenty-one, from Stranraer, costing £50,000. 22-year-old Dene Shields, yet another striker, was bought from Cowdenbeath for £30,000. On the way out of Raydale were Martin Cameron (on loan to Shamrock Rovers) and Mark Boyd (to

Macclesfield). Former captain Mick Galloway had left in the autumn to join Second Division Stirling Albion, in somewhat acrimonious circumstances after a falling-out with Alexander.

Immediately after the 4-2 defeat at Peterhead, the squad travelled on their delayed winter break to La Manga. The sun seemed to have acted as tonic because Gretna embarked on a second winning spree of the season. All of the remaining fourteen league games were won, with an aggregate score of 54-6 and promotion was officially confirmed at Cowdenbeath with a single goal from Steve Tosh on 5 March 2005 – the first senior British club to gain promotion.

After the game, the players' celebrations were, like the result, rather muted. Just before kick-off, former chairman Ian Dalgleish died suddenly at home, aged seventy-four. As a youth of sixteen, Ian had begun cheering on Gretna right from the start in 1946 and had been one of the group of supporters, aided by the German and Italian prisoners of war, who turned the ground at Raydale into a playable surface. He had joined the committee in 1962 and was chairman until 1996, bringing Ron and Helen MacGregor to the club. Mileson arrived at Cowdenbeath that Saturday lunchtime expecting excitement and antici-pation, but was instead met with hushed silence which he initially put down to nerves. The news was not broken to the players and coaches until after the game, and for the remainder of the week leading up to his funeral the following Friday, the whole town was in mourning. Mileson promised that when the new ground was built, there would be a stand named in his honour.

After a minute's silence the following week, the team resumed the job of securing the league championship. After avenging their earlier defeat at Peterhead, Gretna romped to a 6-1 victory over their nearest rivals on 19 March and extended their lead to thirteen points with six games left. The title was finally won on 9 April with a 7-0 thrashing of Stenhousemuir. The week after, Alan Main, one of the big signings from the previous summer, finally got his chance to play in goal in the league, although he was unable to keep a clean sheet. Still, the two goals he conceded were cancelled out by the six scored by his teammates and nothing went past him in the remaining three games.

Gretna finished the season with 98 points from a possible 108 – twenty ahead of Peterhead and forty-seven in front of third-placed Cowdenbeath. It was a record, as was Kenny Deuchar's tally of thirty-eight goals in thirty games. In addition, Deuchar had equalled Jimmy Greaves' record of six hat-tricks in a season, earned while playing for Chelsea in 1960/61. The team had scored 130 goals in the league, only two short of Hearts' longstanding record set in 1958. Other awards included Third Division Manager of the Year for Alexander and SFL Player of the Year (Deuchar again). And just to prove that the big-time billys and fancy dans were actually nice people, it all happened with only one red card and thirty-three yellows.

As the standard of football had increased during the season, there was a direct correlation with the size of the crowd at Raydale. The previous year's average of 465 was almost doubled to 895 and Gretna's was easily the highest in the Third Division, way ahead of the average of 433. Nationally, Gretna had also slowly started to climb the attendance statistics table. In their first season in the Scottish League, they had been fortieth out of forty-two (Montrose and East Stirlingshire had lower crowds), but had jumped now to twenty-sixth, ahead of most of the Second Division clubs.

It was no surprise. It was an exciting time to be a Gretna supporter. Success was almost guaranteed at games where there was a real feeling of joy and camaraderie. Mileson stood in the stands puffing away and chatting to anyone who addressed him. In the director's seats, the MacGregors quietly and tactfully watched their team demolish that of the visiting directors sitting next to them. Spectators stood only inches away from the touchline listening to the players joke with each other like a footballing version of the Harlem Globetrotters, watching the goals pile in. Schoolchildren with complimentary tickets raced around the ground every time the tannoy confirmed the name of the latest goalscorer (more often than not the good doctor or his sidekick, David Bingham). In the dugout, however, Rowan Alexander, joined now by Davie Irons, retained an air of nervousness and professionalism; shouting, remonstrating, cajoling, encouraging, reluctant to accept that any game was over until the man in black blew the final whistle.

Alexander and Irons had been rewarded by Mileson with new five-year contracts – the period of time which would be spent preparing for the Scottish Premier League. Although anything seemed possible for now, there were very few who really expected such an outcome. For the moment, the Second Division was enough. Despite Alexander's caution, it was going to be fun.

5

Stewart Fisher's article in the *Sunday Herald*, where he joked that Gretna would soon have more players than supporters, was centred on the signing of David Bingham from Inverness Caledonian Thistle. Bingham had agreed to a three-year contract, although initially Mileson had suggested five years. 'It's my money,' he dismissively told a bemused Helen MacGregor when she challenged the cost. Mileson had also offered to put both Helen and her husband Ron on the payroll of the club – an offer that was, wisely as it turns out, declined. Fisher's article controversially mentioned a feature for which the growing club would soon be criticised: reaching out beyond its natural catchment. A tactic that all successful clubs embark upon, Mileson was sizing up the area beyond the small township. In linking the expansion with a possible 'rival power base' to steal supporters away from Carlisle, the newspaper was giving voice to a conspiracy theory that would consume many on that part of the frontier for the next few years. Did Mileson intend to wreak revenge against the English side which he was unable to purchase by convincing their supporters to desert across the border? Or, given that even the most cynical of supporters found that impossible to believe (Mileson after all would soon be paying some of Carlisle United's wages and handing over £600,000 to their supporters' trust), was this the first step in an attempt to amalgamate the two clubs? More likely, it was simply a realisation that he could not go on forever pumping money into Gretna and that if the current calibre of player was to continue featuring at Raydale, then additional funding bases (known in the game as 'supporters') would need to be found.

Mileson had certainly continued to pour the cash into Gretna. The accounts for the year show that the loss had jumped by a further £1.9 million, meaning that his personal contribution now stood at nearly £2.7 million. At the start of the 2004/05 season the Scottish Football League had taken an interest in that side of things and told Gretna they could not buy any more players over the age of twenty-one. This was not a rule invented to annoy Mileson, but infuriate him it did, and he spoke openly about consulting a lawyer to challenge the position. The

Scottish Football League no doubt thought that they were doing clubs a favour and had instituted the measure to prevent clubs over-spending on wages and going bust.

Others perhaps wished they had Gretna's resources and would no doubt have eagerly accepted them had they been offered. Many actually welcomed the chance to see someone shaking things up in Scottish football. However, whenever Gretna were deemed to be overstepping the mark and using their cash unfairly, the complaints could be heard. One of Gretna's detractors was Jim Ballantyne, the Airdrie United chairman who had originally lost out to Gretna in his initial bid to join the Scottish League after the liquidation of Airdrieonians. In the summer of 2004 Gretna tried to entice their striker (and future Glasgow Rangers star) Alan Gow to Raydale. Ballantyne was unhappy with the way in which Gretna went about this courtship, which was unsuccessful despite an offer of £100,000 for both Gow and another Airdrie player (named by the *Daily Mail* as Owen Coyle).

Nevertheless, Mileson continued to push ahead with his plans for the club's expansion and this included adding some additional non-playing personnel to the payroll. Graeme Muir was a church elder in Dumfries, where his work on forging community links had come to the Gretna owner's attention. Muir joined Gretna in the autumn of 2004 as community and education officer and began a programme with schools in the area, giving talks and leading training sessions. By November, twenty-seven schools were involved, including some from across the border in

Carlisle. Muir was thirty-eight years old and had been a player with Queen of the South and Gretna in the late 1980s and was full of enthusiasm for his project, often leaving journalists exhausted after an interview conducted at top speed. As part of the schools initiative, children were given free tickets, although they would generally need to bring along a fee-paying adult, and this helped to boost attendance which rose steadily during the season.

Although coaching was Muir's main role, his plans included a book club, sessions for young offenders, bowling games for the older supporters and a new mascot for the club – a rooster subsequently named Rocky, which in turn then spawned a Rocky the Rooster Fan Club for the kids. The desire to engage with the community came genuinely from Muir's Christian ethos – his boss also spoke of keeping the kids 'off the street and away from crime' – but the new recruit also had a shrewd sense of business and understood the financial reasons why Gretna needed to expand and that, without reaching out to the supporters, clubs would end up going to the wall. He spoke evangelically, although with some naivety, of installing popcorn machines to tempt the kids in, and of sending players along to coffee mornings to engage with the public.

Another new recruit with financial nous was Debbie Wicks, who arrived at Raydale in November as commercial director. Having been sales and marketing manager at Carlisle Racecourse, Debbie had been involved in promoting the new Jubilee Grandstand, experience which would no doubt prove valuable as Gretna's plans for a new stadium were drawn up. Rumours began to emerge that the club would have to leave Raydale if they wanted to build a Premier League-compliant ground. The football park lay north-to-south, sitting snug in the corner of two residential streets which ran along the south and east of the pitch. The touchline on the east side was only a few metres away from the pavement outside, with a long covered corridor – nicknamed the bus shelter – providing a little bit of protection against the wind and rain for supporters. There was a bit more space on the south side, which enabled the temporary stand to be erected for the cup game against Dundee United, but essentially the ground was the wrong way round. The only place for increasing spectator capacity was behind both goals.

Mileson spoke of making the club as self-sufficient as possible by introducing new income streams. He knew that he would not be able to go on forever buying top-class players and decided that the way forward would be to develop young talent, hence the purchase of a house in Carlisle for up to nine trainees and the founding of the Gretna Football Academy based thirty miles down the M6 at Newton Rigg College, Penrith in the summer of 2005. The college was then part of the University of Central Lancashire and would later become encompassed within the University of Cumbria. Ex-Gretna player Stuart Rome was then its Head of Football.

Danny Lennon moved from playing to become youth team coach, assisted by Bobby Paterson, while defender Tom Cowan rejected a contract extension offer from

Carlisle United to become Football in the Community Officer at Gretna. They were joined by David Holdsworth who had been injured in August and failed to recover. He eventually hung up his boots but stayed at Raydale as a youth and diet and fitness coach.

The academy built on Gretna's existing youth team structure which had expanded to include teams from the under-11 to the under-19 age groups. Several of the products of this system were, by the end of the season which brought the Third Division title, pushing at the door which led to the first team – notably Danny Grainger and Matthew Berkeley.

As the club and its support grew, so inevitably did its detractors. The common theme was that such a small club with a tiny fan base was living beyond its means, only able to do so because of one man's generosity (which led either to admiration or jealousy) or because of the club's policy of reaching out beyond its hinterland (which led to resentment). Message boards were full of predictions of doom when the money dried up, but equally there was some praise by those who saw Gretna's potential to disrupt the normal order of things in Scottish football, to shake things up a bit. And everyone likes to see a bit of that – unless of course you are one of those being shaken up. Mileson was no novice, no fool. He understood the sustainability argument and spoke openly about it. He also seemed to know what the answer was, hence bringing in people like Graeme Muir (who was soon elevated to a position of non-executive director, and later chief executive) and Debbie Wicks, and the development of a system to replace the older players, with some home-grown talent.

Support came from the local press, particularly the Carlisle-based *News and Star*, where suddenly the team from the English city was in danger of being replaced in the headlines on the back pages. Sports journalist Amanda Little praised Mileson for thinking big and taking pride in trying to run a football club properly, while admitting that crowds of less than 700 meant the club was not self-sustaining. So while the increasing number of fans could marvel at the displays in front of them, off the pitch it was clear that the finance issues were at least openly discussed and were starting to be addressed.

Mileson's wealth, meanwhile, seemed inexhaustible. In May 2005, over the Irish Sea, Shamrock Rovers – at that point Ireland's most successful club – were in trouble. Mileson was reported as being prepared to pump a lot of money into the club to help out in a situation where creditors were owed £2.36 million. Later that month, Mileson dispatched his associate Brian Quigley to Dublin to complete a deal to buy the club. 'It will give Crest a foothold in Ireland and that is what we are looking for,' Mileson told the *News and Star*, referring to the sportswear company he owned. There had already been links between the two clubs. Shamrock Rovers, managed by ex-Carlisle United manager Roddy Collins, had taken Martin Cameron on loan earlier that year and Brooks and Roddy shared some history: Collins had initially been manager of Carlisle United during the time that Mileson had been trying to buy the club and later had a second spell there when John Courtney took over.

The Irish deal fell through in the autumn after Mileson failed to reach an agreement with South Dublin County Council over ownership and tenancy of Rovers' Tallaght Stadium, but the Gretna owner was then subsequently linked with four other clubs there – Bray Wanderers, St Patrick's Athletic, Shelbourne, and, in February 2006, Glentoran (possibly related to Roddy Collins' unsuccessful application for the vacant manager's job).

Mileson continued to give money away to other clubs and trusts. As well as the huge support to both the supporters' trust and club in Carlisle, and the Arab Trust of Dundee United, donations were made to Ayr United's Honest Men Trust, Dundee's Dee4Life Trust, Berwick Rangers Trust and that of Stockport County (where he was made an honorary vice-president). Over the years, it is estimated that nearly seventy clubs in Scotland and England benefited from Mileson and his legacy continued for a while in non-league clubs such as Gilford Park, Carlisle, with its Brooks Mileson Stand or the Brooks Mileson Memorial Trophy in the Northern League.

A psychologist might suggest that he almost seemed embarrassed by his wealth – an 'awful word' he once declared – and determined to pass it on as quickly as possible. While the distribution was wide, in Gretna its concentration would prove to be the cause of a two-year long party, followed by the inevitable hangover.

But all of that was still to come. For now, times were good and one thing was certain; the march was never going to stop simply with accession to the Second Division. At the end of the season, arrangements were made by an independent Edinburgh-based television company, Hand Pict Productions, to film Gretna's progress to an anticipated second successive promotion. Once more expectations were high, and lacked the nervousness of previous years. Gretna would do the business, wouldn't they?

Yet only one player was added to the squad in the summer of 2005, a short cheeky-faced striker who had just experienced a disappointing season with Dundee United. James Grady was then thirty-four but felt he still had a few more playing years left in him and was delighted to join the Black and Whites. Alexander and Mileson's de facto practice was now to bring in the required players during the January transfer window, with the occasional exception. Meanwhile, those going the other way were Martin Cameron, who, after being on loan at Shamrock Rovers, permanently left the club to join Forfar Athletic. Also departing, though this time on loan, were Brian Wake and Mark Eccles (to Scarborough) and Dene Shields (Stranraer).

Off the pitch, with a lack of football to report on before the new season began, the newspapers busied themselves with events relating to the Milesons. Despite continuing to pay the wages of some of Carlisle United's players, Mileson's relationship with Fred Story had deteriorated to such an extent that he spoke of suing the United owner for defamation and libel. Mileson was also involved in a public war of words with the Scottish Football League President, John Smith, after yet another donation to a football fans' trust. This time the beneficiaries were the supporters of Berwick Rangers (to the tune of £10,000) and Smith had enraged Mileson in suggesting that, by trying to be some sort of Lone Ranger, the Gretna owner risked provoking the ire of other clubs who would be voting within a year, at the end of Gretna's probation period, on whether the Third Division champions would be allowed to become a full member. The alternative was face expulsion from the league. This time Mileson was careful to emphasise that his disagreement was a personal one with Smith and not with the Scottish League.

Better news for Gretna fans came with the news that Mileson, recognising that the club essentially relied on his funding, began planning for the future. His son Craig, a talented 28-year-old magician who had worked for his father's other companies, speculatively asked his father if he could come on board at Raydale. Mileson, pleasantly surprised, agreed and started talking about how Craig would take over running the club once he was no longer around.

The other main topic of conversation that summer was about Raydale, or, as seemed more likely, a new stadium at a different venue. The football finally began with some pre-season friendlies including the annual Annan Tournament, from which Gretna were later permanently excluded along with Dunfermline, after both sides were felt to have shown disrespect by sending reserve teams along to the event while their first teams played an alternative match up in Fife.

As was normal practice, however, the competitive season began with a Challenge Cup game, and a defeat at Greenock Morton (3-2 after extra time), who would turn out to be Gretna's main challengers in the Second Division that season. A week later at Raydale, in the first league game against Forfar Athletic, Gretna found themselves a goal behind after fifteen minutes and worried faces began to spread around the crowd and the home bench. The disappointment of the previous week, along with any further anxiety, was soon washed away in the late summer drizzle when Gretna then went on to put five into the Forfar net and begin the season at the top of the table.

After a further two league wins against Raith Rovers and Stirling Albion, Gretna's lack of cup success continued with a narrow 1-0 defeat against Premier League Dunfermline in the League Cup. A stumbled 2-2 draw against Ayr United preceded the important first league battles with the other teams generally thought to be contenders for promotion, Morton and Partick Thistle. In the first Gretna avenged their earlier Challenge Cup defeat with a 2-0 victory in Greenock. The second game was at Raydale, where the stand from the Dundee United game was back in place behind the goal on the south side of the ground.

1,920 fans turned up to see Gretna storm into a 2-0 lead only to lose it with two second-half goals – one a last-minute penalty – and share the points with the visitors. The game, like much of the season's drama, was captured on the documentary being filmed that season, and with which the club – including Mileson, Alexander, Graeme Muir, Debbie Wicks and the players – appeared happy to co-operate. The film captured the growth of the club, on and off field, as it continued at breathtaking speed. Additional office space was created with portakabins being lowered into place on the land to the west of the pitch. The temporary stand was then deconstructed to enable a roof to be put on.

On the film, Mileson is eager to explain what his game plan is. 'It's fun,' he tells the camera, 'this is not one of my businesses… my businesses pay for this.' He reveals that his kids had pleaded with him not to spend all of their inheritance. 'I'm sure I won't do that,' he laughs. But it was more than fun. Mileson really believed in putting something back into the community, hence the free coaching and education classes provided to schools in the area, a programme which he suggested he had a moral duty to provide. These sessions were certainly a hit with the schools, their children and staff. Jane Mitchell from Creetown Primary School describes them as 'music to the ears of a primary headteacher'. Praising the 'good quality' of the classes, she goes on to explain that in her view, this is just the club 'giving back' with no catch – although she does recognise that it is also a clever way for the club to gather in more supporters, and at a young age.

The draw with Partick was followed by seven victories including another over Morton in which Ryan Baldacchino scored the goal of the season so far when he chipped the keeper from almost the halfway line. Another draw with Partick and five more wins took Gretna to Christmas Eve, eleven points clear at the top and an unbeaten run of thirty-one games. The Christmas presents arrived in the form of Team of the Year awards from the BBC *Off The Ball* team and a similar one from journalist Chick Young, who named Mileson as his 'football man of the year'. The Gretna benefactor was also presented with the *News of the World*'s Big-Hearted Sportsman of the Year title at a ceremony in Glasgow and Rowan Alexander picked up his second Manager of the Month award since the start of the season.

It was something of a shock then when the league leaders lost 2-1 at home on Christmas Eve to Forfar, their first home league defeat since April of the previous year. Rowan Alexander detained his squad for an extra hour after the final whistle to deliver what must have been an interesting festive message.

Gretna would recover in the New Year with a twelve match unbeaten run which included twenty-five league points from a possible twenty-seven, but, as was now customary, the January transfer window gave Alexander the chance to revamp his squad. Three new players came in. Arriving from the First Division were the Stranraer captain Allan Jenkins (aged twenty-four, midfielder) and defender Martin Canning (also aged twenty-four) from Ross County, midfielder John O'Neill joined from Falkirk. Andy Aitken left to sign for Queen of the South, while a number of the youngsters were sent out on loan, including Matthew Berkeley (to Workington Reds), Danny Grainger (Brechin City), Brian Wake (Hamilton Academicals – he had up until then been loaned out to Scarborough) and Bryan Gilfillan (Stranraer).

Of the additions, only the cost of Canning was published at the time: £60,000. Ross County had previously turned down a lower bid as clubs understandably sought to do as well as they could out of Gretna's seemingly bottomless pit of cash. Gretna also tried to prise Northern Irish international Peter Thompson from Irish League Linfield. An initial bid of £50,000 was turned down. Further offers more than doubled this but in the end Gretna withdrew their offer when it became clear that Linfield's valuation was higher.

Not that money seemed to be a problem, although Gretna were keen to emphasise that the main outlay was on wages (and endless win bonuses), rather than transfer fees. Before the opening of the January 2006 window, Alexander pointed out that he had only spent around £150,000 on such fees. Just before Christmas, *FourFourTwo* magazine published its Football Rich List. Mileson had been placed at number forty-nine with personal wealth of £36 million, ahead of the chairmen, directors and owners of clubs such as Aston Villa (Doug Ellis, £26 million),

Everton (Bill Kenwright, £21 million), Leeds (Ken Bates, £30 million) and Newcastle United (Douglas Hall, £20 million). Mileson was starting to be spoken off in the same breath as the Lithuanian owner of Hearts, Vladimir Romanov, who with £200 million was considerably richer than the Gretna owner but was also making a name for himself as being one of Scottish football's unconventional figures. Chick Young had described Romanov as 'nutty as a fruitcake'. On the other hand, Romanov's view of journalists could be viewed in the Hearts programme notes where he accused journalists, amongst others, of being 'driven by the Devil' and 'seeking to ruin all that is good about the game'.

However, not everyone was happy with the way things were being run at Gretna. In January Debbie Wicks decided to leave. Although Miles praised her and said she would be missed, and Debbie herself said she would continue to come to Raydale as a spectator to support the club owned by the man she described first and foremost as 'a friend', she also made the point that she did not like the restrictions placed on how she could do things and how she was told not to get involved with certain aspects: 'Lines were drawn in the sand.' She loved Gretna Football Club, but not the way it was run. Graeme Muir simply, and perhaps rather disparagingly, noted that the club was on a journey and not everyone would make it the whole way.

Among the results pleasing the ever-increasing throng of Gretna fans, were successes in the Scottish Cup. For once, the Black and Whites were doing well in a knock-out competition, progressing past the first and second rounds with victories over non-league teams Preston Athletic (6-2) and Cove Rangers (6-1). As with the English FA Cup, the big teams enter at the third round. A year earlier, Gretna had lost admirably to Dundee United; this time around they were drawn against First Division St Johnstone and Steve Tosh scored against his former employers, the only goal of the game, to take Gretna to a fourth round tie at Clyde.

That game, played on 4 February, was a bad-tempered goalless affair with captain Chris Innes sent off for the visitors while Clyde lost Alex Williams and Chris Higgins. In an attempt to calm the situation and spread some love, red roses were handed out to the women who attended the replay at Raydale on Valentines Day, and the romance continued with Gretna winning the game 4-0 and securing a place in the last eight of the competition.

The quarter-final was a much more nervous affair against St Mirren. A crowd of 2,850 turned up at Raydale to see Kenny Deuchar fire the home team into the semi-final of the cup with a single goal. As the fans realised they would be going to Hampden (for real, as opposed to an away game against Queen's Park), they sang with joy. Mileson did too: 'It's just so much fun!'

By the 7 March, after a 3-0 win at home against Dumbarton, Gretna were fourteen points clear of second placed Morton with ten league games left. The following Saturday, Gretna would bring that second successive title much closer if they could beat the Greenock team at Raydale. A good support from Morton in the new stand taunted the home crowd when, after a lacklustre seventy-eight minutes, the visitors eventually opened the scoring. Two minutes later it was 2-0. As we stood shocked in the bus shelter stand, my son Rufus, then aged eight, began to get upset. An elderly gentlemen turned round all smiles and sympathy and offered us one of his boiled sweets. 'Ach, it does them guid to get their erses kicked once in a while,' he chuckled. 'They'll still win the league by the end of the month.'

He was right. Morton faltered and, with successive victories over Partick Thistle and Ayr, on 25 March Gretna came back from a goal down to win 2-1 against Alloa. The Gretna players walked off the pitch, aware that their performance had been well below par despite the victory, but surprised by the cheering crowds. Someone shouted that Morton had lost 4-0 to Ayr. Then it became clear: Gretna were champions. It had taken them three weeks longer than the previous season, but winning the title and promotion before Easter was still some achievement. And once again, the decisive goal came from Steve Tosh.

There was still the important issue of a semi-final to be played at the national stadium. A week after winning promotion, Gretna travelled to Glasgow to take on First Division side Dundee. To an extent, Gretna's detractors were right to point out that throughout the cup run, they had managed to avoid a team from the Premier League and that the Old Firm had both slipped out at the earlier stages.

Rangers had lost to Hibernian, who would be contesting the other semi-final with their Edinburgh rivals, Hearts. Celtic had been eliminated by First Division Clyde – but it was Gretna who had, in turn, then sent them packing. Gretna also defeated St Mirren and St Johnstone, First Division winners and runners-up respectively, so while it hadn't been the hardest of journeys to Hampden, it was no breeze either.

On Saturday 1 April 2006, on one of the many supporters' buses heading to Glasgow for the game, a copy of the *Daily Record* was handed round. An article was being read about the latest proposals for a new ground. This time the story was that the stadium would be part of a new marina to be built on the shore of the Solway. In fact, the football field would technically be 'offshore' and, so the article said, this would enable Mileson to take advantage of a loophole in local government legislation and mean he could puff away on his 100-a-day cigarettes, despite the recent introduction of the anti-smoking laws. The April Fool was clever – even containing the views of an alleged Dumfries councillor, Alf Poolir, who, while generally supportive of the Gretna owner, was worried about 'thousands of cigarette butts washing up on the shore' – and it certainly provided some light relief on what was going to be a very tense day. More telling was the fact that one of Scotland's biggest daily newspapers chose to run the story in the first place. It was a sign of the rising level of fame of the club and its aspirations, and of course, of Mileson himself.

The game was screened live on terrestrial TV, but that didn't stop thousands of fans turning up in black and white colours to cheer on the Second Division champions who, the bookies declared, were favourites rather than the team from the higher league. As well as the prize of a place in the Scottish Cup Final, the game had by now taken on an added edge.

The previous summer, Rowan Alexander had spoken about his dream of taking Gretna into one of the European competitions. Having then just won the Third Division title at a canter, talk almost naturally emerged of what he would do if another club came with a job offer. 'I have everything here at my fingertips, so there's no reason I would want to move elsewhere,' he explained. 'There are some exciting times ahead and the biggest test of my career will be when we're in the SPL and aiming to get into Europe. That is definitely obtainable.'

Indeed it was. By January the bookmakers were offering odds at 250-1 of Gretna playing in the UEFA Cup by 2009-10. There is no record of how many punters took up that option, but by the time of the semi-final those odds looked incredibly attractive. The reason for this was that the rules of entry to European competition in Scotland stated that whereas the Premier League winners and runners-up would qualify for the Champions League, the third-placed team and the winners of the Scottish Cup would go into the UEFA Cup. By winning the cup, Gretna or Dundee would make it into the draw for the following season's UEFA Cup. However, if the winners of the Scottish Cup had already qualified (by finishing in the top three in the league), then the team losing in the cup final would enter the UEFA Cup too, albeit at the second qualifying round.

With Hearts then sitting in second place, a win by them in the other semi-final would mean UEFA qualification for the winner of the Gretna-Dundee game – providing that Hearts did not slip up in their last few league games.

Gretna and Dundee kicked off at lunchtime and the first goal arrived on the stroke of half-time, courtesy of Kenny Deuchar's boot, squeezed over the Dundee goal-line from an almost impossible angle. After fifty-seven minutes, Gretna were awarded a soft penalty when Bobbie Mann was judged to have brought down Ryan McGuffie in the box and McGuffie completed his unique style of penalty kick (walking away from the ball, turning quickly and shooting almost without looking) to make it 2-0. Dundee's lack of luck was emphasised when a dubious shot from O'Neill deflected off the legs of Barry Smith for an own goal. The scoreline of 3-0 was perhaps a bit unfair on Dundee, but the better team had won and would be returning on the 13 May, the first team from the third tier to make it to the final in the history of the competition. Hearts did indeed book their place as opponents by thrashing Hibernian 4-0 the following day.

With only the mopping up of the last few league games before the big day out (four wins and, surprisingly, two defeats – to Forfar, again, and Stirling Albion), press coverage inevitably concerned itself with what Gretna had achieved so far, and asking where it would all stop. Articles appeared in the *Guardian* and other national media concentrating on the two personalities who made the club – the manager and the owner. As ever, opinions were mixed. Picking up on the fact that Mileson had been helping to sell semi-final tickets from Raydale's makeshift ticket office and would do so again for the final, the *Guardian* described him as: 'the kind of club owner who actually believes in the quaint notion of football clubs contributing to the community around them, as opposed to paying lip service to the concept; the kind of club owner who spends money giving the club's young players the basis of a university education so that if the manager decides one day the kid is not good enough to make it he will have something to fall back on; the kind of club owner who finances drug education programmes and employs five full-time coaches to tour the local schools using football as a teaching aid; and, finally, the kind of owner who has made somewhere in the region of £50 million in the insurance business and, after two heart attacks, one broken back, one removed kidney and a nasty case of ME, has decided it is time to share the wealth.'

On the other side of the coin, even hitherto supporters like Chick Young were beginning to question the wisdom and fairness of allowing a Second Division team into Europe at the expense of Premier League clubs who had finished sixteen or so places above them in the league. Others highlighted again the money issue. How much would the Gretna team's win bonus be? Was it really going to be £10,000 each as per one of the rumours doing the rounds? Had Kenny Deuchar really been promised a £60,000 Jaguar XK if he scored the winning goal? Once again the issue came round to Gretna's resources, although there was little discussion about Hearts' money. The wage bill of one their players, Craig Gordon on £12,000 per week, was not much less than the amount for the entire Gretna team.

Even a good news story about Mileson buying tickets for 1,000 children from the club's schools programme was turned around by some as an attempt to fill what would be Gretna's embarrassingly empty section of the ground. But there was no need to fear such an outcome with over 12,000 turning up at Hampden to cheer on Gretna (Hearts had the bulk of the other 40,000), thus leading to that question: 'Where *did* they come from?'

In Gretna itself there was a party atmosphere. Shops and businesses, such as CSW Insurance, filled their window displays with posters, scarves and good luck messages. Then there was the song.

The Hugh Trousers Band had released their first album 'Old is The New Black' in 2005. Referring to themselves as a 'collective with a changing line-up', the band, whose lead singer was David McCallum, the Blairgowrie branch manager of an insulation company, agreed to re-record the third song on the album which was called 'Living The Dream'. McCallum had heard Mileson use the title in an interview and offered use of the song. So, following one of the British cup final traditions, a new version was produced in April and released in time for the big day and actually made the Indie Chart Top 30. To be fair, it's no cheesier than many such cup final songs and at least it had the credibility of having been written for a different purpose and with supporting vocals from Sam Brown (who had sung with Pink Floyd and Jools Holland). Nevertheless with lines like, 'I got the Doctor by my side... soaring like an eagle,' the chance to ridicule was not lost by some.

As Rufus and I sat with friends in the stadium on 13 May, watching Alexander and Mileson down below, I suspect many of us were simply hoping not to witness an embarrassing defeat, aware that workmates (mainly Carlisle United fans) and others who had not bought into the success story were willing exactly just that. For the first few minutes we held our breath as Hearts' attacks seemed relentless. The post was hit; Alan Main made a terrific save from Skacel. Then another from Jankauskas. Then from Bednar.

Hearts took the lead near half-time – after thirty-nine minutes – when Skacel picked up a long throw-in from Neilson and put the ball easily into the net from a few metres out. Having got to only 1-0 down at the interval, Gretna seemed to grow in confidence and became, to our surprise and delight, the stronger side, following a tactical decision to change from 3-5-2 to 3-4-3, replacing midfielder Davie Nicholls with striker David Graham. Steve Tosh had a chance and then David Graham's nearly-goal would have been one for the telling had he not been robbed by Neilson after dribbling round the Hearts keeper.

In the seventy-fifth minute, John O'Neill was brought down by Cesnauskis in the box. Ryan McGuffie's penalty kick was initially saved by Craig Gordon but he picked up the rebound and put the ball into the net. After that both sides had chances to win the game, but the score remained 1-1 right through thirty minutes of extra time. I looked around the crowd. Many were nervous, but like Alexander, as he went from player to player on the pitch encouraging the chosen penalty-takers, there were also smiles. We felt like we had done it. We had held a Champions League team in the final of the Scottish Cup. The game would now be decided on the lottery which is the penalty shootout, but to a certain extent, that didn't really matter. We had not lost the game.

Except, of course, that it did matter. Five brave souls from each team would now volunteer to play their part in bringing the game to a conclusion. Sadly both Gavin Skelton and Derek Townsley, players who had been with Gretna in non-league days, were the two who missed and the trophy went to Edinburgh. Nobody was harsh on the losing side. Praise from Alexander and Mileson was echoed on the car radio as we drove back down to the border and would even be heard in offices in Carlisle in the next few days. Chick Young was back on side too: 'They say that no one remembers beaten finalists. That no one is interested in second prizes… Sorry, not this time. Gretna have just blown that old wives' tale out of the water.'

The magnanimity went both ways. Mileson paid for a half-page advert in the *Edinburgh Evening News* the following week to thank the Hearts fans for their generous support and standing ovation towards the defeated Gretna players. The cup final smiles continued. There was much to look forward to: UEFA Cup and First Division football next season, where Gretna were already one of the favourites for promotion to the Scottish Premier League. Mileson had immediately shown his continuing support for Alexander and Irons by offering renewed five-year rolling contracts. Once again the season had ended with much to look forward to, although beneath those smiles there was a growing anxiety about the speed of success and some of the problems ahead.

6

Financial losses, which came hand-in-hand with foot-balling success at Gretna, continued despite the cup run. The accounts up to 31 May 2006 show an identical in-year deficit as per the previous period: £1.9 million. This meant that the club now owed a staggering amount of debt built up over the previous three years. The sums owed were £4,950,000 to Heartshape Ltd (owned by Mileson) and £400,000 to the man himself. The accounts noted, with not much comfort, that as repayment of these 'loans' would not be requested before 31 March 2008, the club would be able to trade *until at least that date*. In short, whereas before the success of the club was put down to the generosity and support of one man, now that generosity was confirmed simply to be a loan, and the existence of Gretna FC clearly depended totally on him. Whatever Mileson said in the press about providing support beyond his grave through his son Craig, and whatever trust funds he was apparently setting up – and there was no reason to doubt his word on this – in reality, the financial position of the club was extremely precarious.

The amounts owed were huge, but they still seemed affordable for a man whose wealth was now being quoted at being around £75 million. No one doubted Mileson's passion for the club (surely if he left, he would just write off the debt?) and few questions were asked publicly. Instead, Gretna ploughed on with remedies for another major problem which would soon be standing in their way: Raydale Park.

Gretna's football ground had undergone some significant refurbishment in the past decades and would be barely recognisable to those prisoners of war who had flattened out the pitch nearly sixty years before. The club had purchased most of the remaining land which ran alongside Dominion Road up to the main Annan Road in the north in 1963, land which housed the social club and the one-time bustling Sunday market. However the football club and social club were often barely on speaking terms, suspiciously eyeing one another across the rough car park which now needed stewards on match days to prevent collisions between vehicles and the ever-growing number spectators. Ron MacGregor had identified the need to try and repair relationships in 1996, but it was an ongoing issue.

In 1982, prior to joining the Northern League, £100,000 had been spent on upgrading Raydale Park and a new stand was built along with floodlights and changing rooms. Ten years later, another £50,000 was needed to prepare for the Scottish Football League – a job done well, but in haste, leading to accusations of the club being fleeced by the firms who took advantage of their predicament and requirement to get things done quickly.

Although no worse than many non-league and lower division club facilities, with Mileson's arrival and the growing expectations of further progress, there was continuous talk of a new stadium. In July 2003, after the first season in Scotland, Mileson was telling the local press about plans to spend more than £1 million on upgrading the ground to a '4,000 capacity luxury stadium'. There would be three new all-seater stands (no room to replace the 'bus shelter' on Dominion Road), new public bars, five-a-side pitches and so on. Architects were already drawing up plans and work would begin in the summer of 2004.

A year later nothing had really progressed other than that plans had now developed to talk of a 5,000-seater stadium costing £3 million. This would be a 'modular build' which would enable capacity to be further increased to meet the Scottish Premier League's requirements of 6,000 seats should success on the field lead that way. The press release at the time even went so far as to name the contractors (Ken Hope from Carlisle) and noted that a group called Sports Facilities International was involved. Mileson's exuberance about the project, however, was tempered with his all too common disparaging comments about the pre-Mileson Gretna – 'a club that was dying on its feet' – which did not help the rift between the club and some members of the community that continued despite his limited efforts to increase fan participation. Although Mileson was an enthusiastic supporter of trusts at other clubs, during his time at Gretna he made only limited attempts to reach out to his club's own supporters' group, which would formally become a trust in 2007. Nevertheless, on this occasion he made it clear that he wanted to involve the people of Gretna in the new stadium. 'I want [it] to become an asset the community can be proud of,' he told Amanda Little. 'I don't own Gretna FC and I want it to be part of the area instead of the community always being at loggerheads with the club. There has been a terrible feeling between the club and the community in the past, because, I think, of a lack of communication.'

While there was no doubting his sincerity, sometimes his lack of tact and appearance of steamrolling ahead with what he thought was best, discarding those who disagreed with him, left mixed emotions with the fans. They were, mostly, grateful for where he was taking them, but sometimes one could not help feeling annoyed with this newcomer's negative and disparaging remarks about the past, or worried about whether his apparent autocracy (despite the denials of being the owner) would ever be capable of healing the wounds in the town that had built up over the years.

A fear shared by all football supporters is just how committed are those in charge of their own particular club. In the case of Mileson it was clear that he was willing and able to throw cash at Gretna, but would the resources he was providing lead the club so far up the ladder that if he disappeared the fall would result in the most severe injury? Or was he going to be true to his word and not only build something for the community, but also ensure, as he promised, that it would be left with enough of a legacy to continue when he did eventually step away? He was certainly aware of what the team was achieving with his backing, and of the need to provide some permanent and appropriate infrastructure for what was now a European competition club. Graeme Muir, the chief executive brought in by Mileson, described Gretna as a 'fast-moving train with no station to stop at', a metaphor which clearly brought to mind the eventual outcome which might happen if nothing was done to prevent the train crash, either by slowing down the train or building that station.

By 2006, the new station option – a new stadium – had taken on even more significance for Mileson. It would become a litmus test of his commitment and of how serious he was about the club's journey. Was he a temporary joyrider who would someday abandon the club or was he there for the long term?

Back in August 2004, Gretna fans were on the whole pleased with the reports that Mileson was unhappy with the plans the architects had drawn up, taking this as evidence that he wanted the job done properly. He ordered the work to be redone with a timetable that meant everything in place by summer of 2005. However, a year later, there was still little change at Raydale and talk was now about a move to another site. The site of the new ground was to be revealed at the end of July, but the deadline came and went with nothing other than a statement from the club that a 'local landowner of high integrity, who also has the community at heart' was involved. To preserve the quality of Raydale's playing surface, training took place in Annan at the council-owned and grandly titled Everholm Stadium, but once the new ground was built, training would switch back to Raydale. In the autumn the club had brought back the temporary south stand, which would increase the crowd capacity to around 3,000, bringing income which would help to narrow the sustainability gap at least.

However, there was some disquiet among the fans. One wrote to the local paper asking why Mileson was spending £600,000 on the Carlisle United Supporters' Trust when he should be upgrading Raydale. As for finding somewhere to build a new stadium? 'I'll believe it when I see it.' Nevertheless, the club appeared to continue to take the matter seriously. There were visits to Bolton Wanderers' Reebok Stadium to look at matchday organisation, although Bolton's average home crowd of over 25,000 was somewhat out of Gretna's range. Plans were also said to include a crèche for players' children and learning and health centres for the community.

Having toyed with the idea of relocation, the talks with the landowner 'of high integrity' came to nothing because, by March 2006, a redeveloped Raydale was back on the agenda. This time, there would be 6,300 seats and the cost had increased to £5 million.

The issues surrounding Raydale had by now reached the national press with the April Fool's Day story about an offshore stadium appearing in the *Daily Record*. Finally, by the summer of 2006, words began turning into actions. Discussions took place with the Premier League and other footballing authorities, not least because Gretna had a UEFA cup home tie coming up soon and Raydale would not be suitable for that game. As for the possibility of the club winning a third successive promotion and knocking on the door of the Premier League, Gretna were told that although they would need to have their ground ready by the 31 March preceding the season in question, the club would be allowed a period of grace if things were not quite finished, during which they might be able to share facilities with another club. The problem with Gretna's geography, however, meant that the nearest Premier League-compliant ground was around seventy-five miles away at Motherwell, a journey of commitment which would surely test even the most die-hard fans. Nevertheless Motherwell publicly stated they would be willing to offer the hand of friendship (along with a bill, no doubt) to Gretna.

By the end of April, there was some real news. Planning permission to move the pitch northwards to enable a bigger south stand had been applied for and during the summer months the old north stand was torn down and taken away. Meanwhile the details were being finalised and would be submitted to Dumfries and Galloway Council by the end of the summer. As ever, the town's opinion about its football club was divided with objections being lodged by a small number of residents who felt that Gretna's football team was outgrowing its home town.

At the end of August, just before the plans were due to be considered by the Annandale and Eskdale Area Committee of the council, the application was pulled to enable some of the traffic concerns to be addressed. Frustrating as it was for everyone, Graeme Muir nevertheless insisted this was a temporary tactic and the consideration would go ahead in September. To the collective relief of all involved at Gretna, it finally happened on 25 September 2006.

The plans submitted mentioned that this would be the first phase of the club's proposals. The capacity of the ground would be increased by erecting two stands with a seating capacity of 3,048 each, on the northern and southern ends of the ground, and to install new floodlighting. The south stand would be for away fans, the north for home. Traffic measures included a new access point on Dominion Road which would not be used on match days. Instead visitors would enter from the Annan Road to the north. As expected, the club had reached an agreement with the nearby greyhound stadium to share car-parking facilities on match days.

The plans were supported by the council's officers and by the police, Scottish Water and Environmental Health. The Scottish Environment Protection Agency also gave their approval, although this would be dependent on an agreement regarding surface water drainage before building work commenced. There were six objections put forward by local residents, mainly related to concerns about traffic and policing. To them the proposal represented a material change in the intensity at which the football club had operated. In short, the club was getting too big (the new stadium would be able to hold all of Gretna's population and still be half-empty) and this would attract anti-social behaviour. The objectors made reference to the club's own previous public pronouncements that Raydale was unsuitable for a stadium this size.

On the other side, public support came from those who pointed out the benefit to local businesses of the rise of Gretna FC and a petition, organised by the supporters' club, was submitted containing 701 signatures. A traffic assessment submitted on the club's behalf by architects Barron Wright pointed out that in reality crowds would be much lower than the final capacity of 6,400; in the First Division they were more likely to be around 2,500.

It was unexpected, therefore, when the councillors decided not to give their final approval to the application and asked for some further details and a site visit. It meant that the club would probably miss the March deadline for Premier League compliance, although there was still the ground-share option. Two site visits were made, one on Tuesday 10 October and another for the home game against Clyde on 21 October (an exhilarating 3-3 draw with a crowd of 1,118). On Monday 23 October, the Annandale and Eskdale Area Committee considered the application again. This time there was unanimous support although the club was 'strongly advised' to set up a local residents' forum which could 'meet on a regular basis to discuss and wherever possible address and resolve issues of concern resulting from the activities of the football club'.

Everything now seemed set for the push towards Premier League football. During the summer there had been further additions to the squad. Brendan McGill, a 25-year-old fleet-footed Irish winger moved from Carlisle United on a free transfer. McGill had turned down Gretna two years previously but was now enticed by the prospect of more security and European football. Neil MacFarlane, a 28-year-old midfielder, joined from Aberdeen, while young defender Craig Barr arrived from Blackburn Rovers. Leaving Gretna were Dene Shields (to Stirling Albion) and Bryan Gilfillan (Peterhead).

Gretna's ambitions were illustrated by the appointment of their league-winning reserve coach, David Holdsworth, to the new post of Director of Youth Football, and the establishment of a women's team. More significantly, despite Rowan Alexander and Davie Irons signing new five-year rolling contracts, the Gretna supporters were more than a little bemused in early July to hear that they

now had a new Director of Club Development. Mick
Wadsworth had been manager of, among other clubs,
Carlisle United, Scarborough and Huddersfield Town.
He had also managed abroad – at Beira-Mar in Portugal
and national coach of both St Kitts & Nevis and the
Democratic Republic of Congo – and had worked for
the FA, as a regional and then national coach at under-
21 level. As part of the England setup he became a good
friend of Sir Bobby Robson and the pair had also worked
together at Newcastle United, when Wadsworth was assistant manager.

Perhaps unintentionally, Wadsworth's confidence,
relayed in his brusque Yorkshire accent, came across as
verging on arrogance and he had a history of annoying the
fans of the clubs he worked out, leading to the setting up
of one legendary website which branded him 'football's
biggest bastard'.

Mick's first act after arriving at Raydale was to tell
Helen MacGregor that he would be organising his own
press release. 'I've been in discussions with Gretna for a
long time to shape a role that is most beneficial to the
club,' he told the local paper. 'I'll be using my experience
to help in all areas, from the youth team to the first team.
I'll be helping Rowan Alexander, Davie Irons and David
Holdsworth to be the best they can be. I'll help move
Gretna FC forward to bigger and better things.' Initially
at least, the line being given was that Wadsworth was
there to help with the development of the entire club;
footballing affairs would be left to Alexander and Irons,

although they would no doubt be looking over their shoulders at the more experienced 55-year-old and his offers of assistance.

Wadsworth arrived in time to watch the first pre-season friendlies, which included an astounding 18-0 victory over South of Scotland League team Threave Rovers. Despite eleven goals being scored by Kenny Deuchar, Gretna continued their pursuit of Shrewsbury Town's striker Colin McMenamin, previously managed at the Shropshire club by Wadsworth. McMenamin, who had also played for Annan Athletic (at that time managed by Davie Irons), Newcastle United (assistant manager – Mick Wadsworth) and Livingston, signed at the end of July.

The day after the annihilation of Threave, Mileson was taken to hospital with a burst bowel. The manager of the hotel in Gatehouse-of-Fleet, where Brooks and wife Gerry had been enjoying a short break, calmly tried to keep the Gretna owner conscious, despite heavy blood loss, while the ambulance arrived. An emergency operation was needed to save his life and he went on to recover slowly from an exhausting summer. As well as everything going on at Raydale – the new signings, Wadsworth's arrival, preparations for the UEFA Cup match – Mileson had endured a series of blackouts and a resulting brain scan. There was also a trip to Westminster with the MacGregors, local MP David Mundell and Jim Sheridan MP, chair of the All Party Scottish Football Group, for a Parliamentary discussion about football in the community.

As the new season started, it was another politician with the name Sheridan who hit the headlines. The MSP Tommy Sheridan had just won an action for defamation against the *News of the World* newspaper and awarded £200,000 in damages. As he emerged victorious from the court, he described the outcome as a David versus Goliath moment. 'It was like Gretna playing Real Madrid at the Bernabeu and defeating them – on penalties.' Sheridan's joy was actually short-lived. In 2007 he was charged with having committed perjury in this case and convicted in 2010.

A Gretna game against Real Madrid was now a possibility. To get to the Spanish capital would require, amongst other results, a victory over Irish side Derry City in the club's first UEFA Cup game.

7

New signing Colin McMenamin sat on the Raydale bench on 5 August during the first league game of the 2006-07 season and wondered if he had made the right decision in coming to Gretna. He, and nearly 1,700 others, watched as the home side demolished Hamilton Academicals 6–0. Sure, he was happy for his new club, but based on this showing, would they ever need him? Steve Tosh had just scored a hat-trick. Brendan McGill would get two. McMenamin made his debut after seventy minutes with the score already at 5-0.

Gretna started at the top. 'That's the season over then,' muttered one departing Hamilton fan to another. 'What do you mean? We'll recover fair enough,' replied his companion.

'Aye, we will,' said the first one. 'We can play better than that. But wha's gonna stop *them*?'

Five days later, Derry City were given the chance to do just that when they introduced Gretna to European football. The prospect of such a game taking place had actually been raised by Rowan Alexander over a year earlier when he talked about the then Third Division champions being in the Premier League and the UEFA Cup. Fanciful it may have seemed at the time, but for Alexander this was 'definitely attainable'. Once Gretna's place in the tournament was confirmed, there was a backlash from other clubs who felt that this would prove to be an embarrassment for Scottish football: Jimmy Calderwood, manager at Aberdeen (who had finished fourth in the Premier League and therefore missed out on European football) was particularly annoyed, a sentiment that found sympathy even with the normally loyal Amanda Little at the *News and Star*.

The game took place at Motherwell's Fir Park and was watched by over 6,000 fans, including a large contingent who had travelled across the Irish Sea. Gretna started well and after Ryan McGuffie put Gretna ahead after twelve minutes, the 'home' fans began their customary, if annoying, chant of 'Easy! Easy! Easy!' Ten minutes later Derry had equalised and scores were level at half-time.

After the interval, Derry took control and scored three goals in nine minutes to make it 1-4 with nearly half an hour still to play. Fortunately the Irish side slowed down. The resulting 1-5 defeat for Gretna did, after all, seem to justify those who had declared the event would be embarrassing for the Scottish side. Gretna's European dream was over almost as soon as it had begun. There was still an away leg to play and the Scots did at least salvage some pride with a much better performance and a 2-2 result, but there would be no trip to the Bernabeu – at least not this year. The BBC's Chick Young, while not heaping any blame on Gretna, summed it up by noting that the borderers 'were out of their depth as surely as if they had waded out into the Solway'.

Rowan Alexander's wrath after the first leg yielded and turned into praise following the second. The team had shown 'great spirit' and deserved a pat on the back. Alexander had decided on a three-man attack in an attempt to claw back the four goal deficit but to no avail. Without doubt Mick Wadsworth, the new Director of Club Development, was taking notes.

At least this defeat meant Gretna could now concentrate on the league and the team got back to winning ways only three days after the 5-1 defeat with a 2-1 victory over Clyde. By the end of August Gretna had played eight competitive matches: four league wins, two Scottish Challenge Cup wins and the two Derry games. They had scored thirteen league goals (six of which came courtesy of a relieved Colin McMenamin) and conceded only two. Going into September, Gretna were top of the league by two points and it was no surprise when Alexander and

McMenamin were given the First Division Manager and Player of the Month awards respectively. Only three weeks after the horror of Fir Park, the UEFA Cup was long forgotten.

The last of these league victories, 3-0 at Gretna's self-proclaimed new rivals Queen of the South on 26 August, was particularly sweet for Rowan Alexander. This was the club which had humiliatingly dumped him as manager seven years earlier, a fact that some of the Dumfries supporters were keen to point out as he walked towards the dugout before the start of the game. Never mind that Alexander had previously presided over some success at the club, including taking Queens to a Challenge Cup final; these days he was seen as some sort of 'traitor' along with Gretna's physio Kenny Crichton who had also worked at Queens. To add further impetus to the visiting team's desire to win, the stuttering tannoy out bleated out versions of 'When Irish Eyes are Smiling' (a reference to the Derry games) and 'Big Spender'. Rather predictably, at the final whistle when Alexander rushed onto the pitch to hug his players, the home supporters colourfully expressed the remainder of their dissatisfaction.

All teams, even the most successful ones, come to expect a dip in form. For Gretna this started in earnest with the visit of Dundee on 9 September. A 4-0 home defeat at Raydale was followed two days later by being knocked out of the Challenge Cup by fellow First Division side Ross County, 3-2 after extra time. The next league game saw

Livingston visit Gretna and both teams struggled towards a 1-1 draw.

Gretna then suffered their biggest defeat since entering Scottish football, albeit inflicted by Premier League team Hibernian. It was a League Cup game in Edinburgh which saw Alan Main pick the ball out of the net half a dozen times. His counterpart in the Hibs goal, Zibi Malkowski, was hardly troubled. The final score was 6-0.

The post-mortem that followed the match was a turning point in the development of the club. Mileson described it as a 'salutary lesson' and a marker to how the team would perform in the Premier League. From that point on, the club accelerated its plans to prepare for the future, rather than just one season.

Gretna's performance picked up briefly and spectacularly with a 6-0 victory over Partick Thistle, but then came a 2-0 defeat against Airdrie and two 3-3 draws against St Johnstone and Clyde. The last game in October saw Gretna visit the team they had trounced 6-0 on the opening day of the season. This time, as their despondent departing supporter had predicted, Hamilton played much better and Gretna travelled back down the M74 with a 3-1 defeat having taken the club down to fourth place in the league.

Off the field there had been a number of interesting developments. The film crew from the previous season had returned to record what had initially looked like a strong possibility of an unprecedented third successive promotion and league title; at the same time sports jour-

ANTON HODGE

nalist Andrew Ross, an exiled Ross County fan, was often to be found at Raydale, or chatting with the Gretna fans at away games as he researched a book which he hoped would also record success for the club.

Part of the remit given to the normally stony-faced Mick Wadsworth when he joined in the summer was to scrutinise the future sustainability of the club. Gretna's ambitious but costly youth programme was the first victim of such scrutiny and, despite only having been appointed to his new role in May, David Holdsworth was made redundant, along with Viv Busby, in September. On 1 October, the *News of the World* rumoured that Gretna's entire youth setup faced the axe, and confirmation of sorts came a few days later with the sacking of Tom Cowan, the recovering Lee Maddison (despite earlier promises) and Danny Lennon. At that point the salary costs alone for this part of the club were £300,000. Two of the five youth teams were disbanded, although these two (the under-13s and under-15s) were actually not based in the Gretna area. The dismissals led to challenges by at least three of the players, whose redundancy payments originally only amounted to three weeks' salary, and Maddison in particular was very upset. 'I feel I've been stabbed in the back,' he told Amanda Little. 'I haven't had a single phone call from anybody at the football club since this happened. They said they would look after me after I had my leukaemia but they're just words now. It just seems to have been forgotten about.'

Wadsworth, however, was unrepentant. 'Brooks will always be the focus and force behind this club, but it has to sustain itself. I've seen people throw money at football clubs and it all goes backside up. But that's not going to happen here because we've a good man in charge.' When the accounts for 2004-05 were made public in November, showing the first of the £1.9 million annual losses, Graeme Muir admitted that while the debt was nothing to be concerned about, the directors were already looking at how the club would be structured in the future. The £1.9 million was, he said, 'investment', although looking around Raydale, it had in fact bought little more tangible than the temporary south stand and the demolition of the old north stand.

Still, two championships and a lot of fun were nothing to be sniffed at. Gretna's form picked up again during November with four successive wins against Dundee, Queen of the South, Livingston and Partick. The comprehensive 5-0 drubbing of the neighbours from Dumfries was watched by nearly 2,200 fans, including a group from along the coast who kept their spirits high with a continuation of the verbal onslaught against Rowan Alexander. The result put Gretna back on top of the table where they remained for the rest of the calendar year with victories against promotion rivals St Johnstone (2-0), Ross County, Hamilton and Dundee (all 1-0). The only stumble was a defeat at Airdrie who were rapidly turning into Gretna's 'bogey team', despite their position at the bottom of the table – a bit like Forfar Athletic the year before.

As Christmas approached, talked turned towards what might happen during the January transfer window. Kenny Deuchar, the hero of seasons past and the scorer of eleven goals in one game a few months earlier, stunned the club with a transfer request at the beginning of December. Dr Goals, as Sky Sports presenter Jeff Sterling named him, had only managed one in the league so far. He last started a game on 28 October at Hamilton and had been taken off at half-time with Gretna losing 2-0. Since then he had been an unused sub against Dundee and had come on after seventy-seven minutes in the game against Queen of the South (with his team already 5-0 up). He had not featured in the squad at all for the remaining games. When Mileson spoke of his disappointment yet seemed willing to let his one-time favourite go, the fans knew that this would only be the first of some significant changes in the weeks and months ahead.

The next shock came shortly afterwards when veteran Steve Tosh was told he could go for financial reasons, despite having played in nearly every game of the season so far. James Grady was also told he was free to leave if he could find another club, whereas the young Australian midfielder, Erik Paartalu, was offered (and accepted) a two-and-a-half year contract.

The transfer window opened with Gretna sitting eleven points clear at the top of the league and the buying, selling, dismissing and swapping began. Tosh moved to Queen of the South, along with 32-year-old Jamie Mc-Quilken. Kenny Deuchar joined Northampton Town on loan until the end of the season. Mark Birch was loaned to Conference side Southport and another veteran, Derek Townsley, left Gretna for Workington Reds. Meanwhile Colin McMenamin was given a two-year extension to his contract and 21-year-old ex-Manchester United youth player Steven Hogg joined the club. This was another example of Mick Wadsworth's influence as Hogg, a left-sided midfielder, had been at Shrewsbury during Wadsworth's time there. Rowan Alexander confirmed that this signing illustrated the route the club was taking: 'He's another youngster which shows we're looking ahead to the future.' Grady, meanwhile, had decided to stay and fight for his place.

The happy new year began with a 4-0 victory against Queen of the South in Dumfries and a third round win over Clyde in the Scottish Cup. Ominously however, this meant another cup trip to Edinburgh to play Hibernian in the fourth round, just four months after losing 6-0 there in the League Cup.

Despite being 2-0 ahead after seventy seconds at Partick Thistle, Gretna could only come away with a draw from that game, although three points were taken from a 4-1 victory over Livingston a week later.

On 23 January, Amanda Little stunned the world of Scottish football by reporting that goalkeeper Alan Main had rejected Gretna's offer of a one-year contract extension and had signed a pre-contract agreement with the team's main rivals St Johnstone, who had allegedly offered three years. Main had previously been a hero at Saints, having spent eight years there. Nothing was denied or confirmed by either club and the whispers would go on for a few more weeks. More importantly, with Gretna twelve points ahead of their challengers from Perth, the two teams were preparing for a crucial match against each other at the end of the week.

On that day, as the crowd took their seats at St Johnstone's McDiarmid Park, the visitors were once again forced to listen to another club DJ's selection of music being streamed through the tannoy. This time the songs were anything with the word 'money' in the title. As the players warmed up to Abba, Pink Floyd and others, a new face could be seen popping out of a Gretna tracksuit. This belonged to Xavier Barrau, a French midfielder who had just bought himself out of his contract with Airdrie. Listed on the team sheet simply as 'A. Trialist', the 24-year-old was, unbeknown to the Gretna fans, the source of some friction at the club. Alexander would later defend Barrau's inclusion as 'a last-minute opportunity which arose' but unlikely to happen again. Mileson, meanwhile, seemed agitated and annoyed by this, unconvinced by his manager's unilateral decision. More interesting was the fact that Alan Main was to play; either this was a result of the keeper's devout professionalism or it was, as most of the visiting supporters hoped, confirmation that Amanda Little's article was incorrect. However, after only nine minutes of the game, Kevin James put St Johnstone ahead and the home fans' rendition of the England World Cup song 'Football's Coming Home' – changed to 'Main is coming home' – was, perhaps foolishly, acknowledged by a wave from the man picking the ball out of his net.

The rest of the game was scrappy, both sides nervous, although the home side had the better of it. After seventy minutes, the trialist Barrau came on and equalised for Gretna with only six minutes remaining courtesy of a strike from thirty-five yards. The Gretna fans went wild – all except Mileson who remained in his seat – and a fight nearly broke out between the occupants of the two dugouts. Within a minute, St Johnstone had retaken the lead and this time the police had to intervene between the two coaching teams. The game ended 2-1. Gretna were now nine points ahead, St Johnstone had one game in hand and the two had one more meeting left in April at Raydale.

Then came the chance for a break from the league with the second visit of the season to Hibernian's Easter Road stadium in the Scottish Cup. This time Gretna acquitted themselves much better, returning with a harsh 3-1 defeat but a much better performance from a team filled with youngsters such as Danny Grainger, Craig Barr, Matthew Berkeley (who scored) and, in goal, Greg Fleming.

In the next few days another new player was added to the squad, former Newcastle and Motherwell defender David Cowan, who had been released by Ross County. One old-timer who was not willing to give up easily was the 35-year-old James Grady who had come on as a substitute against Hibernian and nearly scored, and was now determined to fight his way back into the team. Grady did make another substitute's appearance at the next league game, at home to Airdrie, but even he could not inspire his team mates and the game ended in a 0-0 draw. A week later Gretna were back to winning ways with a 4-1 victory over Ross County but the next game, defeat to Clyde 0-2, reduced the gap at the top of the table to ten points, and St Johnstone now had two games in hand.

March began with the fourth and final league game against Queen of the South at Raydale. Having beaten their neighbours 3-0, 5-0 and 4-0, Gretna were clearly favourites, although Queens were bottom of the table and fighting for their lives. During the preceding week, web forums had been fanning the flames of animosity between the two sets of fans. Those from Gretna were perhaps a little bit too arrogant; their neighbours on the other hand remonstrated at Gretna for having spent money they themselves would no doubt have gladly accepted. In fact, Gretna's cost cutting had continued with the departure of local DJ Dave Dee, who had been in charge of the matchday radio station, and press officer Jon Tait, whose book *The Team That Dared To Dream*, which detailed the team's games from Third to First Division, was about to be published.

Alan Main was again picked despite the resurfacing of rumours that a statement was soon to be made by St Johnstone. When Stephen Dobbie scored the Doonhamers' first ever senior goal against Gretna after thirty-eight minutes, the home support turned on their one-time hero, shouting that he could have done better. Conspiracy theorists had a field day with the visitors' second goal, scored again by Dobbie when Main miskicked the ball straight to a Queens player in the sixty-ninth minute, and the third – a free-kick from Eric Paton which left Main flailing, albeit there had been a deflection.

It took Rowan Alexander an age to appear in front of the press after the 3-0 defeat and when he did, his suit was soaked. 'Well, it's not champagne,' he replied when asked, but would elaborate no further. It took some weeks for the full story of the incident in the changing room to emerge, although it was never confirmed. It appears that after the final whistle there was an altercation between Mick Wadsworth and Alan Main. Alexander, upset about the result but more significantly about what he saw as his players' lack of effort, allegedly told Main that there was no way he would play for Gretna again then departed the dressing room in tears. Mileson and Davie Irons then tried to calm Alexander down and a meeting was arranged at Mileson's house with all of the coaching and managing staff.

On Monday 5 March, the news that David Bingham was to leave the club on loan to Stirling Albion was somewhat overshadowed by confirmation that Alan Main had indeed signed a pre-season contract with his old club from Perth. Main was then officially suspended from the club and Polish goalkeeper Zbigniew ('Zibi') Malkowski, who had been close to boredom when he played for Hibernian as they defeated Gretna 6-0 the previous year, signed on loan from the Edinburgh club.

On 6 March there was further revelation when Gretna announced that Rowan Alexander was now officially on sick leave for an unspecified illness. While the words used in the announcement and accompanying media interviews were as expected, praising Alexander for his achievements and wishing him well, it was not clear whether this was going to be a temporary or more permanent situation. Davie Irons would be in charge of the squad for the rest of the season, although many fans assumed this would itself only be a stop-gap before Wadsworth fully took control.

There was some good news that evening – Queen of the South's revival continued with a 1-0 win over St Johnstone meaning that Gretna's lead remained at seven points and Saints now only had one game in hand.

Gretna's next game was played on the following Sunday on a miserable and nervy afternoon in Dundee. Grady kept his place for the third successive game and Malkowski made his debut in goal, winning over the Gretna fans by saving a penalty. Final score: Dundee 0-1 Gretna. At the end of the game, the Gretna players, restored to a 4-4-2 formation after weeks of playing with three strikers under Alexander, made a deliberate show of unity with Davie Irons. Rumours now emerged of the rest of the squad applauding Alan Main the week before when he allegedly told Alexander to 'fuck off'.

The show of unity was coupled with more positive news coming from Raydale, including the prospect of signing former Scottish international goalkeeper Rab Douglas should Gretna win promotion to the Premier

League. Then another new youngster joined the squad, ex-Newcastle United midfielder Nicky Deverdics, who had been released by the English Premiership side and had since been playing in the Northern League with Bedlington Terriers. Again, the acquisition of the nineteen-year-old had something of the hand of Wadsworth behind it, the latter having been interested in the player for some time.

Meanwhile, since the granting of planning permission to redevelop Raydale back in late October, once again nothing appeared to be happening. Despite the considerable expense and energy put into achieving such permission, it wasn't long before whispers began doubting the club's intentions. In November, various newspapers repeated the rather unconvincing rumour that the redevelopment project would be shelved in favour of a ground share with Queen of the South. By March, it was announced that Brooks Mileson would meet Scottish Sports Minister Patricia Ferguson to discuss plans for a new community-integrated stadium, which would not be suitable for the Raydale site. Talks were continuing with Motherwell about a possible ground share for the following season and Gretna formally submitted an application to the Premier League on this basis as required by the end of the month.

After a 1-1 draw at Livingston, Gretna's lead was down to seven points, which was further reduced to four after St Johnstone beat Dundee, but with Gretna not playing that weekend, it was the Black and Whites who now had a game in hand. The season was coming to a close: Gretna had six games left to St Johnstone's five.

On 31 March, Gretna moved closer to promotion by beating Partick Thistle 2-0 at Raydale, while St Johnstone lost at home to Livingston. Gretna then played their game in hand, midweek at Airdrie, but their jinx team stifled them and Gretna left with one point and a 0-0 draw. The maths was interesting. With four games left and Gretna now eight points ahead, the following Saturday's fixture meant that a win for Davie Irons and his team would win them the league. That fixture was against St Johnstone in Gretna.

Raydale prepared itself for the celebration, which seemed to be a formality. Balloons and flags were handed out and entertainers laid on for the kids. A number of reporters and celebrities were in attendance, including Chick Young and, accompanied by his old mate Mick Wadsworth, former England and Newcastle manager Bobby Robson, who joined the players in the home dressing room for a pre-match talk. Next door, St Johnstone manager Owen Coyle was using this very fact to add body and motivation to his own speech: Gretna clearly expect you to buckle and let them win, he said, perhaps holding one of the 'SPL here we come' balloons.

When the game started, it was obvious that St Johnstone were angered by the circus and they turned that emotion into a decent display. Gretna began well but by half-time the Trinidad and Tobago international Jason Scotland had scored twice for Saints. In the second half, the visitors were reduced to ten men when Filipe Morais was shown a second yellow card, but this had no impact on Gretna's ability to claw back some ground. When Jason Scotland was substituted after eighty minutes, he received a standing ovation from both sets of fans. A section of the home-based support was calling for Alexander's return and some openly questioned what they saw as Wadsworth's wisdom in clearing out some of the players whose experience might have been useful that day.

The gap closed further over the next few weeks and meant that the final weekend began with Gretna one point ahead of St Johnstone, and with a superior goal difference (+29 compared with +22).

The final games would see both Gretna and Saints playing away from home on Saturday 28 April: Gretna would be at the other end of the country, playing against Ross County in Dingwall; Saints would be at Hamilton. If Gretna won or if St Johnstone drew, the title would be going to Raydale (assuming Gretna did not lose by more than seven goals). If St Johnstone won, then Gretna also needed to win.

The atmosphere in the Highlands was electric and typically combative. Ross County needed to win to have any chance of avoiding relegation and a capacity crowd of 6,216 filled Victoria Park – 10% of whom were visiting fans. A few weeks earlier the St Johnstone manager had been able to rely on the overconfidence and carnival atmosphere at Raydale to bolster his team talk. This time the faux pas came from the Perth club, whose chairman

Geoff Brown had spoken to the press about how Gretna would bring little to the Premier League. His team's promotion would be better for everyone concerned. As for Mileson, any criticism of whom was always likely to stir up the very loyal Gretna players: 'It's his money. But at the end of the day, it's false.'

The drive across the length of Scotland was serene yet nervous, underneath a cloudless late spring sky which was still blue by the time the Gretna supporters – among them Rowan Alexander – reached Dingwall. There was some delay getting over the Kessock Bridge, just north of Inverness, while some poor soul debated whether to jump off or not, which meant the game started five minutes late. Brooks Mileson had travelled against his doctor's orders and sat with his son, Craig, and usual attendants including Jack Gas, who ran the Gretna Sunday market, ex-Gretna captain Mick Galloway and journalist and author Andrew Ross. Everyone looked already drained even before a ball had been kicked.

Play was, to repeat a cliché, end to end, with both teams desperate for all three points. Just after half past three, news came through that St Johnstone were already 2-0 up at Hamilton. Somewhere between the games, allegedly at Braemar, a chartered helicopter was on standby, ready to bring the First Division trophy to wherever the victors awaited. After thirty minutes of play in Dingwall, it looked like the helicopter would be flying south when Michael Gardyne scored for Ross County from twenty yards out. However, four minutes later Gretna's Nicky

Deverdics had equalised and then James Grady justified his own commitment and the club's faith in him by putting Gretna ahead. At half-time the scores were 2-1 to Gretna and 3-1 to St Johnstone: good enough to send Gretna to the top flight.

Then, within four minutes of the restart, Ross County scored, sending despair rippling through the visiting supporters. A couple of friends accompanied an ill-looking Gretna owner out of his seat and away from the crowd while Gretna tried desperately and dangerously to score the winner. All three substitutes were used, all combinations tried. There was a murmur of hope when word spread that Hamilton had scored to bring them back to 3-2, having at one point been 3-0 down, but almost immediately hopes were dashed with the news first that St Johnstone had scored again and the game had ended 4-2.

At Dingwall, as a result of the bridge closure, the game continued beyond the usual 4.45. Gretna tried again and again, throwing everything up front, leaving themselves exposed at the back. In goal, Malkowsky made save after save and punted the ball up the other end of the park hoping his temporary teammates would be able to make use of it. Next to me in the stand, Rufus was in tears as he watched Grady, McMenamin and others somehow fail to get the ball in the net. 'How long?' he asked me. I looked at my phone. 'We're in injury time now.'

The entire visiting support gave a collective groan and held its breath as Mark McCulloch raced in on Zibi, only for the Pole to make what looked like would be the last save of the game. However, with great urgency and some desperation, Zibi booted the ball upfield and Baldacchino skilfully kept it in play. Somehow, in what seemed like slow motion, the ball travelled via McMenamin and Graham to the feet of James Grady, who slipped it under the sliding body of the Ross County goalkeeper and into the net. At Hamilton, the expectant St Johnstone players, forced to hang around for seven minutes after their game ended, received the crushing news that Gretna had scored. It still wasn't over. The Dingwall match had to be restarted and there was another minute of play, during which the home side almost scored – twice!

The whistle blew and, just before 5 o'clock, confirmation flashed up on the television screens throughout the land – Gretna were champions, making history with three successive promotions, their latest triumph being achieved in a style worthy of the climax of a Hollywood movie. At Victoria Park there was pandemonium. Supporters, players, managers (Alexander joined in too), club officials and owners danced around. Even Mick Wadsworth smiled – for a second or so anyway – and the helicopter was cheered as it landed just outside the ground carrying the silver prize. Mileson recovered enough strength to hold the trophy in his outstretched arms in front of the singing visiting crowd.

'SPL, we're having a laugh,' sang the squad in reference to the many times they had been taunted with those words by fans of opposing teams who mocked Gretna's ambition. The club had openly spoken of not being quite prepared for the leap to the top division but, ready or not, Gretna had now made it. The changes during the season, including cost-cutting and concentrating on bringing in younger players, showed that they were making progress. There was still the issue of Raydale, and extra resources would now need to be diverted into working with Motherwell to take over their ground for Gretna home games, and of course there was the matter of who would be managing the team in the Premier League. But for the moment, on a sunny afternoon in the Highlands, such thoughts were temporarily banished from the minds of the fans whose joy was echoing around the ground and up into the cloudless blue sky.

8

Preparations for the new season began almost immediately; it was as if the madness of the rush to the top tier of Scottish football had been prescribed to continue at the same pace lest any slowing down bring the whole club back to some kind of reality. That reality was of a tiny club now about to face the likes of Rangers and Celtic, playing games 'at home' some seventy-five miles away, with no one quite sure how long the owner's beneficence would last, who would be in the team, who would be leading the team.

One person who seemed certain of the last of those issues was Rowan Alexander. In the days after the victory in

Dingwall, the man who had led the club long before Mileson had visited Raydale was suddenly back in the public eye. A few days later, when Gretna's reserve team lost at Raydale, ironically to a St Johnstone team which featured first team manager Owen Coyle, Alexander was there as part of a carnival where the First Division championship trophy was displayed, meeting the fans and marshalling 'his' players towards anyone in the crowd with a camera. He said he would be the person to siphon through the team, deciding 'who we want' and who would be let go. After all, he explained, that was what he had been up to these past few weeks, watching players who would be able to compete in the Premier League.

But Mileson was quick to set out his own version of events, stressing that Mick Wadsworth had actually been in charge of the scouting programme and downplaying any immediate return for Alexander – whose departure would, he once said, cause him to reconsider his own position at the club. Now he was openly saying that there had been no option but to relieve Alexander from his role of managing a team which, he said, had 'virtually disintegrated'.

While Mileson continued to mull over the issue of Raydale – a meeting was set up with the First Minister Jack McConnell to pursue the idea of a 'community stadium' at an alternative site – the changing of the guard began almost immediately. Davie Nicholls, John O'Neill and Matthew Berkeley were all released in the first week of May, while the remarkable story of James Grady's rehabilitation resulted in a stay of execution for the veteran who was now surrounded by a much younger group of teammates: the average age of the squad, thirty-one at the start of the season, had now dropped to twenty-five. Grady would later that summer turn down the chance of moving to Clyde where he had been promised the assistant manager's post in support to the ex-Scotland captain Colin Hendry.

As a Premier League club, Gretna would now be a more attractive prospect to both potential sponsors and targeted players. First, however, there was an annoying hurdle to jump, set up by challenges from the Premier League's bottom teams St Mirren and Dunfermline – the latter of whom had by now been relegated. A meeting of the SPL on 17 May considered the objections raised by these two clubs. The case hinged on whether Gretna had proper plans in place to get Raydale ready in time for a possible second season in the Premier League. The appeal, not incidentally supported by the St Mirren manager, which seemed at the time to taste of sour grapes (and echoed the protests of a year earlier when Gretna had legitimately leapfrogged other teams into the draw for the UEFA Cup), was rejected by the SPL. Gretna's application to play for one season in Motherwell had already been accepted and was confirmed by the committee, although Gretna were reminded that should they intend to remain in the Premier League, they would have to submit a second application by 31 March 2008.

With no remaining obstacles in the path of the tiny but speeding juggernaut from the border, sponsorship deals were announced, players signed and ticket prices hiked up. The sandwich chain Subway signed a deal worth nearly £100,000 to have their green and yellow logo clash with the white shirts and ticket prices were announced as £20 compared with the old price of £12. For so-called 'premium' games (against the Old Firm) the price would increase to £24. Season tickets would also increase from £196 to £355. With a 150-mile round journey, the price of attending a home game might be over £50 for a Gretna fan, although no doubt some would travel in the coaches which were to be run by the newly-formed supporters' trust, a redesigned and reconstituted supporters' club. Graeme Muir also dismissed any concerns about a negative impact of the costs – which seems, in hindsight, a little naïve at best. The trip, he said, would take less time than that which some commuters made every day in Glasgow. How much of a comfort that was to the fan from Gretna is debatable. The club would, in any case, look to fill the stadium with fans from the Motherwell area; Gretna were hoping to become everyone's second-favourite team. Finally, using a scenario that would come back to haunt him, the problem with Gretna's new and yet-to-be-built stadium, Muir declared, was that it would only be able to welcome 6,000 spectators. This would limit the away fans, such as those from Celtic and Rangers, to only 3,000. At least Motherwell's Fir Park would be able to hold many more from those clubs, 'as many as they want.'

The new players began to arrive. First came ex- Carlisle United midfielder Paul Murray (about to turn thirty-one), who, like many of the recent arrivals, had already played for Mick Wadsworth. The next recruit was Ghanaian-born Abdul Osman, a 20-year-old midfielder from Maidenhead United (and also ex-Crewe and Watford). He was followed by a Uruguayan midfielder, the 24-year-old Fabian Yantorno, who had played for his country at under-21 level. From Real Mallorca in Spain came the French defender Aurelien Collin (age twenty-one) and his compatriot, striker Mickael Buscher (twenty) joined from Nice. Gretna had always claimed to be an international club, both Scottish and English, but suddenly that was being taken to a new level. The final outfield player to join – for the moment – was Evan Horwood, a 21-year-old defender on loan from Sheffield United.

Gretna still faced some goalkeeping decisions. Alan Main had gone and the new favourite, Zibi Malkowski, had not stayed on. This left only the young 19-year-old Greg Fleming and a search for additional cover began in earnest. The former Sunderland and Wrexham keeper Michael Ingram was given a trial in a pre-season friendly with Welsh champions The New Saints, but in the end only 19-year-old Nathan Wright was signed from Darlington. The real target for Wadsworth (for it was the Yorkshireman who was now effectively in charge of recruitment) was Tony Caig, who had been at Carlisle from 1991 until 1999 (Wadsworth had been the manager there between 1993 and 1996), until being sold just before the transfer deadline and had subsequently played in the Premier League with Hibernian among other teams. Now thirty-three, Caig had recently returned to his home county of Cumbria after a spell with Vancouver Whitecaps in Canada. Yet there was a problem in that Caig had effectively broken his contract by returning early and discussions continued between the clubs and the SPL to find a way around this. When the transfer window closed at the end of August, Caig had still not been able to sign for Gretna and it looked like Greg Fleming would be the number one choice (but given the number 24 squad number). As a last resort, 37-year-old Colin Scott was also signed – despite the fact that he had been forced to retire from Queen of the South in the summer with a knee injury.

In the middle of June, news broke that Davie Irons was to be head coach. Derek Collins would be the assistant, while Wadsworth would be given a new role as Director of Football. Effectively, Irons became the public face of the club, but Wadsworth's experience would be there to help. A compensation agreement finally brought to an end Rowan Alexander's story with Gretna.

The new squad met and in their first games demolished opposition from the South of Scotland League: a 5-0 win over Dalbeattie Star from a side featuring the new striker Fabian Yantorno was taking place while up the road in Kirkcudbright, a different group of players were hammering St Cuthbert's 10-0. The remaining friendlies saw mixed results and the last first team game to be played at Raydale for some time ended on a sour note with a

2-0 defeat by Morton, two weeks before the start of the season.

As the opening day crept closer, Gretna continued their search for another goalkeeper – Caig's return to the Premier League looked no nearer – with talk of bringing Zibi back, or even signing Vito Mannone from Arsenal. There were mixed messages about the club's ambition. While potential recruits from top English side Arsenal were mooted, at the same time the club pulled out of purchasing Derry City's Darren Kelly citing the £50,000 fee as being too high. Money was certainly going to be tighter – Mileson had decided not to renew his shirt sponsorship of Workington Reds – but the expectation that Gretna were going to bring in a good number of players to see them through the first season in the Premier League before consolidating the next year and playing back in (or at least nearer to) Gretna, did not really materialise.

On Saturday 4 August, TV cameras were positioned outside Fir Park to capture a staged piece for the sports bulletins involving some of Gretna's younger fans. Instead, the TV crew was delighted when they were told that Rowan Alexander was on his way, intending to enact a small drama of his own. Accompanied by his agent, Alexander attempted to make his way into the stadium only to be turned away very publicly. Immediately, he released a statement:

> Today, as the manager of Gretna FC, I attended Fir Park, Motherwell to do the job I am contracted to do. My repre-

sentative, Kevin Drinkell, and my solicitor, Mr Leo Martin, have made numerous and repeated attempts to clarify and resolve my situation currently with Gretna FC, without success. As a friendly suggestion from Brooks Mileson, I took some time away from my role. Throughout, there has been nothing medically wrong with me. However, I have been requested by the club to stay away. Today I am here to celebrate Gretna's achievements as the manager who has guided the club to a Scottish Cup Final, into European competition, and through three divisions to the SPL.

It was an embarrassment and a diversion before Gretna's all-important first top-flight game. The response from Gretna was swift. Captain Chris Innes questioned his ex-boss's sanity in 'coming to an SPL team at two o'clock in the biggest game of their career and trying to do what?' Another former club captain, Mick Galloway, a constant matchday presence at the side of his friend Brooks Mileson when he wasn't playing elsewhere, finally went public over his bust up with Alexander in the following day's *Sunday Mail*. In an article headed 'Alexander Treated Me Like a Dog and Claimed I was a Piece of Cancer', Galloway declared he was not surprised by Alexander's stunt. His ex-boss had, he alleged, called him 'an infectious piece of cancer' which was particularly insensitive given that Lee Maddison was then recovering from the disease. Alexander's treatment had caused Galloway to become depressed: 'I just hope Rowan reads this and knows how much he affected my life … He treated me like dogshit on his shoe.'

To no one's surprise, message boards began to fill up with others weighing in amid allegations of bullying. One poster who claimed to be the father of a former youth player at Raydale put it succinctly: 'I have never come across a human being who I found so vile.' The club reacted by threatening disciplinary action against the former manager and accusing him of bringing the name of Gretna FC into disrepute.

In the midst of all this, there was a rather historic football game being played. After three successive promotions and only five years after gaining entry to Scottish League football, Gretna were now in the top division in the land. Sadly the players were soon handed a lesson in just how hard it would be to remain there.

A disappointing – and frankly disappointed – crowd of 2,731 witnessed the first game against Falkirk. It would be the highest home league attendance of the season, excluding games against the Old Firm and their landlords, Motherwell. Gretna started well and nearly took the lead twice in the eighth minute when new Falkirk goalkeeper Tim Krul won a one-on-one battle with McMenamin, and then Yantorno's shot was parried away by Jack Ross. But after thirteen minutes Michael Higdon had headed the visitors into the lead and he scored again ten minutes later. In the second half the gap was doubled with goals from Pedro Moutinho and ex-Ranger Russell Latapy.

Davie Irons now had to shoulder the burden for the club of appearing in front of the TV cameras, a requirement of playing with the big boys, and explain his side's performance. His assessment that the players would learn from the experience of a 4-0 defeat was overshadowed by the prospect of a visit to Hibernian the following week.

Up in Edinburgh, despite being dominated by the home team, Gretna found themselves 1-0 up at half-time courtesy of a set-piece free kick from Fabian Yantorno. In the fiftieth minute, Colin McMenamin added a second goal and the Gretna fans held their breath. Their team could not hold its nerve. With twenty-six minutes to go, Hibs' Zemmama pulled one back and two minutes later it was 2-2. With the game looking to end as a draw, Hibs kept pressing and in the eighty-third minute they took the lead. Insult was added to injury when McCann scored a fourth in stoppage time sending Gretna back down to the border with a 4-2 loss.

The promise that the team had shown in Edinburgh was further developed with a return visit to Edinburgh for the next game. This time, against old cup final opponents Hearts, Gretna came away with their first Premier League point after a 1-1 draw. Successive defeats to Motherwell (2-1), Rangers (4-0) and Kilmarnock (2-1) left Gretna clear favourites for immediate relegation back to the First Division. There had been one victory – a League Cup win, 3-1, over Second Division Cowdenbeath. A paltry crowd of 342 turned up for that one.

On 22 September at Fir Park, Gretna faced Dundee United, a team who were hoping to go joint top of the Premier League should they dispose of the Black and Whites. United scored after nine minutes and Gretna fans were once again looking forward to witnessing Irons' usual post-match interviews, where his demeanour and body language tried hard not to give the impression that he was fed up with the constant beatings. However, the manager (or perhaps the Director of Football) had revamped things a bit. Craig Barr, Brendan McGill and Abdul Osman had been dropped and into the team came Nicky Deverdics, Erik Paartalu and David Cowan. The last change in particular proved to be an inspired choice. More controversially, Chris Innes had been replaced as captain by Paul Murray – or rather he hadn't quite. Confusing everyone, the manager explained that Innes, a 'great leader', would remain as club captain, but Murray would be 'team captain'. The decision, he insisted, had been his; just in case anyone thought Wadsworth had been behind it.

Whoever had been the instigator, the gamble paid off. At 1-0 down, Cowan equalised and then put Gretna 2-1 up by half-time. In the second half Lee Wilkie made the scores level, but with four minutes left, Allan Jenkins came off the substitutes' bench to score the winner. In the last few minutes (and then some extra time added on), Gretna defended desperately with Cowan heading a certain goal off the line in the dying seconds.

Hopes of a revival proved premature with the next seven league games all lost. Gretna were unlucky to lose 2-1 at Fir Park to Celtic in a game televised live on Sunday 7 October. The underdogs' lead, courtesy of Yantorno the scorer, held until the eighty-seventh minute before two late goals plunged the home fans into despair. It wasn't until a visit from Hearts in late November that Gretna took their points total from fourteen games to a heady five, with another 1-1 share. In December there were further losses to Motherwell and Celtic, but a brief flurry of excitement when, following draws with Kilmarnock and Aberdeen and another victory over Dundee United, Gretna entered 2008 with ten points – a good month's work.

It was during December that Tony Caig finally took over in goal from Greg Fleming. Although Caig had signed for Gretna as an amateur on 6 October, he only played one game that month. Meanwhile Fleming had been called up to the Scottish Under-21 squad and kept his place at club level until the 2-1 win over Dundee United a few days before Christmas.

As colder weather crept in and attendances dropped at home games, the focus on Gretna's plight intensified. The situation wasn't helped by the ejection of three Gretna fans from the game against Inverness Caledonian Thistle on 27 October, a 4-0 defeat with Caig in goal. As the players trooped off at half-time, 2-0 down, Allan Jenkins was subject to some degree of verbal abuse. Jenkins pointed the culprits out to police, but it was only later on in the game, when they started to pick on Davie Irons, that they were ejected. Afterwards, one of them was featured on the Radio Scotland phone-in show and the nation's football fans were laughing once more at Gretna. The bruised head coach, while claiming not to understand why the

fans would want to abuse the team, also began to publicly question Wadsworth's policy of bringing in younger
players: 'From my point of view, I knew we needed some
players with SPL experience who had been over the course
before.' As for the quality of players necessary for that
challenge? 'I think it was underestimated.' However, there
was no need to worry – the club could rely on Mileson:
'He will bring out his cheque book, just as he has in previous seasons.'

The game against Inverness had attracted the lowest
ever Premier League attendance of 1,020. It could, reported the BBC, get embarrassing. Meanwhile, the next
stage of the solution to Gretna's stadium problems seemed
to be talk of an 'eco-stadium' on the outskirts of the village. Any chance of redeveloping Raydale was now being
officially dismissed by the club. Graeme Muir remarked
that Mileson might as well put £2.5 million into a hole
in the ground and set fire to the cash. Instead the planned
environmentally friendly stadium (which would rely on
government support – i.e. Mileson would not be paying
for all of it) would use geothermal under-soil heating and
would catch rainfall to water the pitch. Electricity would
be provided by wind power. Around the land, among
those Gretna had pissed off over the years, the sniggers
were turning to belly laughs.

Even before the January transfer window opened,
Gretna had begun to make changes in the playing squad.
Nigerian striker Henry Makinwa, a free agent, was able to
join in November, while Colin McMenamin was loaned

out to his old club Livingston and Ryan Baldacchino joined Ayr for a month. Kenny Deuchar returned from St Johnstone, having proved with ten goals that he still had the striker's touch. Meanwhile, Rowan Alexander was finally sacked, although he would later claim that he was still owed £800,000 by the club.

During January a number of players left the club as fans' hopes turned towards a revamp which would save them from relegation. Allan Jenkins and Ryan McGuffie joined Morton while James Grady could hang on no longer and moved to Hamilton, along with David Graham, who was now dating a Cumbria lass called Helen Skelton, soon-to-be television celebrity and sister of teammate Gavin. Niall Henderson moved to Raith Rovers, Fraser McLaren to Montrose on loan. Others loaned out were Erik Paartalu (Stirling Albion) and David Bingham (Cowdenbeath). The aged goalkeeper Colin Scott hung up his boots for the second time in a year, while David Cowan went to Dundee (soon followed by Colin McMenamin), and Martin Canning to Hibernian (via Queen of the South). Gretna's most lucrative deal of the month was the sale of Danny Grainger to Dundee United for £30,000.

Evan Horwood's loan deal ended and he returned to Sheffield United, although in an almost straight swap, his teammate Kyle Naughton was sent the other way in what turned out to be the only major signing by Gretna. Deuchar had returned and was looking good but he was joined by a group of unknown youth team players from a number of English clubs in what was clearly a half-hearted attempt to fill the gap left by the departures of fourteen players. The kids loaned to Gretna were John Paul Kissock (Everton), Danny Hall (Shrewsbury), Ben Wilkinson (Hull), Rhys Meynall (Barnsley) and Rostyn Griffiths (Blackburn). Suspicions about Gretna's financial position were not exactly quashed when it was revealed that the 46-year-old Davie Irons and his 38-year-old assistant Derek Collins had re-registered as players.

The day before the transfer window closed there came the most shocking news of all. After all the hassle he had caused for the club following Wadsworth's determination to sign him, Tony Caig decided to leave not just Gretna but the British Isles to sign with Houston Dynamos in Texas. Gretna scrambled for a replacement and ended up with Birmingham City's third-choice Polish goalkeeper, 21-year-old Artur Krysiak.

Caig's last game had been the Scottish Cup replay against First Division Morton. The original game had ended 2-2 after Gretna had taken a two-goal lead. The rematch was played at Queen of the South's Palmerston Park, ending in an embarrassing 3-0 defeat for the Premier League club.

Just before, Gretna had rallied slightly in the league. A narrow defeat at the hands of Rangers was followed by a 2-0 victory over Falkirk, a day remembered for the terrible clash between Fabian Yantorno and the Falkirk keeper, Tim Krul. Both players lay motionless for a few anxious moments before the Uruguayan was stretchered off, his injuries so bad that he would never play for Gretna again. Krul recovered. The Black and Whites were then left nine points adrift at the bottom of the league after two defeats in Edinburgh in the same week, one to each side (Gretna's first loss to Hearts), although the second of these was somewhat overshadowed by the news that Brooks Mileson had been admitted to hospital.

9

Mileson's health had been a constant worry to his family and to those Gretna fans who knew just how much their team depended on him. However, when he was rushed to the Cumberland Infirmary on 13 February 2008 after collapsing at his home, no one was quite aware of where this latest scare would eventually lead.

The rise of Gretna FC after joining the Scottish League occurred at breakneck speed: three successive promotions, a cup final, European football; attendances rocketing, then falling just as hastily; TV documentaries, media headlines, passion, love, support and vitriol spilling across the internet. The rise happened much more quickly than expected – too quickly really.

The speed of that trajectory, when the downturn came, did not let up. In fact, the events over the next few weeks would have confounded anyone who had taken their attention away for even a few days.

On Saturday 16 February, as Gretna warmed up for their 'home' game in Motherwell, against Motherwell, supporters' conversations included the latest angst about Mileson's health, along with speculation that the club might finally be rid of Alexander as he was favourite to replace the departing Morton manager Jim McInally. Alexander, like Davie Irons and Derek Collins, had been a hero at the Greenock club in the past. It presented an opportunity not only for the man to move on, but also for Gretna. Other groups of fans couldn't hide their excitement about the news that Mick Wadsworth would not be at the game: rumour had it that he was in Canada. 'But he's missed the transfer window!' said one. 'Nah, he's looking for another job. Interview with the Canadian FA.' Was this to be another welcome development for some of the Gretna fans?

On the pitch, Gretna went down to another defeat, 3-1, and Irons was apoplectic with rage when his team were denied a pretty obvious penalty. With his ex-boss still in the background and his current one across the Atlantic, it had not been easy for Davie Irons; yet there seemed to be no doubting his commitment as the fans watched him shouting across the pitch at the short-sighted officials and consoling his distraught players as they shuffled back to the dressing room.

A couple of days later, the entire Gretna staff – players, office workers, chief executive – were dumbfounded, then increasingly anxious, when one by one they realised that their pay had not gone into their bank accounts. The problem, it was hurriedly explained, was an oversight. Unusually for a senior football club, all of the sixty or so employees were paid on a weekly basis. The money was transferred not from Gretna FC's accounts, but from one of Mileson's own, and only Mileson could authorise the payment. The businessman's grip on the club and its reliance on him was even tighter than people imagined. As a result of his illness, he hadn't been able to do what he needed to do, whether that meant signing off the salaries, or meeting the Scottish government to discuss the Eco-Stadium plans – a meeting about the latter had had to be cancelled for the same reason.

Although the embarrassed club put the episode down to a blip which would be quickly rectified, the financial position of Gretna was soon the talk of Scottish football. A club that once annoyed others with its seemingly bottomless pockets was now not capable of paying its players. Professional Footballers' Association Scotland commented that it was monitoring the situation while *The Scotsman* questioned why, with Mileson's frequent illnesses in the past, this had never been an issue before. The *Scottish Daily Mail* even reported rumours of the club going into administration.

On Tuesday 19 February, the Morton vacancy was filled and, as predicted, it was an ex-Gretna manager who took the place. It was not Rowan Alexander but, to the shock and dismay of many around the border, Davie Irons. Derek Collins went with him. Mick Wadsworth stepped off the plane from Canada to find himself in charge of first team affairs with reserve coach Andy Smith. Whatever had happened over the Atlantic, Wadsworth confirmed he would remain at Gretna 'for the foreseeable future'.

With Graeme Muir now refusing to rule out the club going into administration, Irons asked the fans to try and see it from his point of view. 'I've had to put my family first and I don't think anyone would blame me for that,' he said. 'With all the uncertainty, I owed it to my family to secure the future.'

Not everyone accepted this. Ex-captain Mick Galloway, who had made his views about Alexander known after the staged appearance on the first day of the season, accused Irons of betrayal in a two-page spread in the *Daily Mail*, which also voiced the question everyone else was asking: what had happened about Mileson's promise a year earlier to ensure that he would put something in place to protect the club's future? 'My son will take over Gretna if something happens to me,' he had told everyone.

The resignation of Irons allowed him to more freely give his side of the story, confirming what many had suspected all along. 'There were times when I felt I was working with both hands tied behind my back … times when I couldn't influence things I disagreed with,' he told one newspaper.

To another he scoffed at the idea that the club had become more sustainable after Wadsworth's arrival: 'The SPL bill is higher than in Division One. I was having to get rid of players while more expensive ones were coming in.' One player had been on £1,500 per week.

Despite this, a few years later the Wadsworth-Irons partnership was almost renewed. In 2012, Carlisle amateur team Gilford Park was renamed Celtic Nation in a story which had some close resemblances to that of Gretna FC. After a chance encounter in 2012, when he stopped to help their team bus which had broken down on the way to a game, USA-based millionaire Frank Lynch bankrolled the club, enabling the non-league team to entice higher quality players including ex-Gretna striker Colin McMenamin and goalkeeper Greg Fleming. In April 2013 it reported that Mick Wadsworth and Davie Irons would be the new lead coaches of the team – Wadsworth was the only one to arrive and stayed for ten matches. In July 2014, Lynch pulled out of the club, leaving finances to last one more season. The club folded in April 2015.

Back in 2008, better news came on 21 February when Mileson was released from hospital. He had been diagnosed with a brain infection and the club reported that with treatment he would make a full recovery. Craig Mileson stressed that his father needed complete rest over the next few weeks, but that staff would be paid the following week as planned, with an extra payment made to make up for the missed one. A meeting between PFA Scotland and Gretna players to discuss the crisis was cancelled and as Gretna prepared for a live TV match against Rangers, it looked like the 'blip' had been sorted.

That game resulted in a not unexpected 4-2 defeat at Ibrox and was followed by the announcement that the scorer of both Gretna goals, Kenny Deuchar, would be leaving the club for the last time. He was off to Major League Soccer in the USA to join Real Salt Lake, where he would play against the likes of David Beckham's LA Galaxy – the two teams met on 3 May 2008 where the game ended 2-2; Deuchar scored once, Beckham twice.

In the midweek game Gretna managed only their fourth win of the season by beating Kilmarnock 4-2, a victory which Wadsworth dedicated to Mileson. The next day, worries resurfaced. Wadsworth told the BBC that Gretna were still experiencing some financial problems: 'Brooks is still ill and the financial lines have been cut at the moment.' Mixed messages continued. Fabian Yantorno was reportedly being offered a new contract, extending his one-year deal which he had signed the previous summer, while rumours of administration continued.

Gretna had been due to play Dundee United at Fir Park on Saturday 1 March, but following heavy rain the game was postponed until the following Tuesday. Then it snowed, so it was cancelled for the second time. The SPL, desperate for the game to be played before the league split into two for the remainder of the season (an oddity which is meant to make the last few games more exciting, but is really the result of having a league of twelve clubs), rearranged for a second time and the game was played at short notice on Thursday. Although Gretna had already claimed the Arabs' scalp, United went home with a 3-0 victory. More worryingly was that, following another lowest-ever Premier League crowd of 501, news began to filter through that the financial situation at the club was terminal.

Hopes had been raised and dashed and raised again throughout the previous fortnight, but this time it looked like there was no way in which the club could avoid going into administration. As Wadsworth criticised the SPL for ignoring Gretna's pleas to postpone the game until a time when more fans would be able to travel, he crystallised his thoughts about the real position of Gretna FC: 'I just hope we can make it to the end of the season.'

The next day, Friday 7 March, representatives from the club met with David Elliot and Lisa Hogg from Wilson Field, a company that dealt with insolvency. Elliot had previously been the administrator at Carlisle United while working for another firm back in 2002. Although Gretna's staff had been paid what they were due, it was clear that there were others who were owed money, not least the Inland Revenue who were threatening to take the club to court to recover a figure reported at £350,000. After mulling over the options during a weekend in which Gretna had no game, the decision to enter administration was confirmed. This would stop the taxman filing for a winding-up petition or provisional liquidation.

The impact on the football field meant that Gretna would lose ten of their sixteen points, leaving them twenty-one behind St Mirren. After three promotions, the shock of almost certain relegation should have had a bigger impact on the fans, but there were clearly bigger issues to worry about.

Gretna were only the fourth Scottish club to go into administration – Motherwell, Dundee and Livingston preceded them – and a number of clubs in England had also gone through the process. Only a few did not survive, but the size of Gretna made the club more vulnerable than most. The key would be the amount of debt and whether it could be repaid. The administrator's main aim was to get the club into shape so it could be a sustainable business, while finding some way of paying back as much of the debt as it could. The club's creditors would be asked to write off part of the debt and agree a repayment plan, but of course there was no certainty they would do that. The Inland Revenue was notoriously difficult in agreeing to provide troubled companies any flexibility.

One thing was certain: Gretna could not keep adding to the debt as they were currently doing. The club was not receiving as much in income as it was spending. Attendances of 501 were only going to provide a miniscule contribution to the rental costs of Fir Park. Then there were other costs such as salaries, which had not been paid for a second time. In the past, Mileson had – or so it had been supposed – been bridging the gap between income and expenditure, but it was looking more and more likely that the once-passionate people's millionaire had already made his last contribution. With Gretna now being run by David Elliot and Lisa Hogg, a statement was made which said that Mileson was '*currently* not in a position to facilitate further financing'. Fans debated whether that meant he had run out of money (the whole £70-odd million?) or that he was just physically too sick to sign the cheques. Others argued that Mileson's family (of whom only Craig was known to have any positive feelings for Gretna) had hidden the chequebook, fearful that the family's inheritance would soon be all gone.

At Gretna, those who had hogged the limelight were suddenly absent from public view and a clearly pained and saddened Ron MacGregor found himself transported back in time to become the face of the club once more. On Tuesday 11 March, he expressed his hopes in most of the national press that his club would not become like Reggie Perrin and disappear into the Solway. There was a feeling that the football club, if it were to survive post-Mileson, would have to radically rethink and reshape how it operated. 'It is the end of the rise and rise of the club,' noted the Chairman, before adding that, 'the future has to be as a small community club.' Mileson and Muir had also used the word 'community' in the past few years, but it now became clear that MacGregor was the only one of the three who actually understood it. Muir's ambition had led to a distorted view about what size that community was; Mileson had failed, despite repeated assurances, to actually engage with it. As the old Gretna FC fell apart, divisions in the community, largely but not solely as a result of some of the actions of the previous six years, would be a potential obstacle to the club's future reshaping.

That evening, my son Rufus and I sat in the bar at Fir Park with friends Graeme and Pete, having travelled to watch the game against St Mirren only to find out when we got there that it had been postponed. There was an over-sufficiency of Scotch pies (not too many though – attendances had been dropping steadily) and as we munched, we talked about the prospects of Gretna surviving until the end of the season and what would happen to the league if they didn't. More importantly, what would happen to our club?

The SPL had said that it would be willing to provide some cash to help Gretna stumble through the rest of the fixture list. The last thing the league wanted was to have to write off Gretna's previous results and recalculate the league standings. The main beneficiaries would have been Dundee United (who had lost twice to Gretna), but as Rangers had played and beaten Gretna three times so far, while Celtic had only played two games, it would have meant that Rangers would have lost nine points to Celtic's six. The result would have been Celtic jumping Rangers to the top of the table, a controversial outcome.

Negotiations took place to advance Gretna some of the cash they would have been guaranteed at the end of the season. The club which finished bottom would receive £720,000 in prize and television money as well as a further £250,000 'parachute payment' to help acclimatise to the First Division (in recognition of the fact that some of their players would be on SPL wages). There would be a further parachute payment of £125,000 the following season, assuming that club did not immediately bounce back into the Premier League.

While all this was going on, vultures began to circle. Carlisle United manager John Ward refused to rule out a raid on the Gretna players, apparently the same view was held at Davie Irons' Morton. Then, to add to the anguish, there was an overnight break-in at the club; among the items stolen were some football boots and fresh meat from the fridge. It was this sad fact which prompted me to email the Gretna Supporters' Society, of which I was a member, asking if there was anything that the society should be doing to help out. In reply, one of the committee members, Steve English, emailed back. What was I willing to offer?

Ironically, going into administration began to bring some long-absent clarity to Gretna's financial situation. As well as the amount owing to the Inland Revenue, it was also reported that two former managers were seeking payments of £800,000 and £100,000 each. This could only have been Alexander and Irons, although at this stage the names were unconfirmed.

Gretna's next game was a long trip away to Aberdeen on the following Saturday, 15 March, but with no news of the requested cash advance, Elliot let it be known that unless £30,000 could be found to cover the cost of the wages and the trip, the game would not take place. He was not sure he would even have a team. 'I can't insist that the players play if they haven't been paid, and I can't pay them on Monday either,' he complained.

I had written back to Steve English and said that I was a qualified accountant – as was my friend Pete – and also did a bit of writing in my spare time. If those talents could be put to use, we were happy to offer them. I hadn't actually checked with Pete at that stage, but I had a hunch he would be willing to help out if he could. Steve replied and said he would be in touch. My email had hinted at the possibility that the club might fold and that a new one could rise in its place, but officially the Gretna Supporters' Society was sticking to the line that the club would remain open.

A number of parties interested in buying Gretna had come forward to David Elliot. One of these was headed by Paul Davies, a football agent, whose father Ken was in charge of security at Gretna. Having looked at the figures, the administrator confirmed that Mileson had put in 'around £8 million' to the club but that was it; there would be no more from that source. The last accounts to the end of 1996 had shown that the club owed nearly £5 million to Mileson's company, Heartshape, and a further £402,000 to the man himself. Mileson had confirmed in March 2007 that he was expecting to have added another £1,106,000 to this figure by the end of July 2007 and then, assuming promotion to the Premier League, another £2,076,000 during 2007-08. That was presumably where David Elliot got his figure of £8 million from. However, in accounts published a year earlier, Mileson had only guaranteed not to request repayment of his funds before 31 March 2008 – a date that was now only two weeks away.

Those in charge at Annan Athletic tactfully expressed their wish to replace their neighbours in the Scottish League should Gretna go out of existence, but the club wasn't dead and buried yet. Former Carlisle United manager Roddy Collins, never one shy with the press, made it known that he and some wealthy property backers from Ireland were interested in buying the club. Although any substance would be dressed up in the flamboyance and hyperbole which was worn by Collins wherever he went, the news was worth taking seriously: he had been the man who had led John Courtney to Carlisle. A meeting was set up between the administrators and the Irishmen for Tuesday 18 March.

The aim of David Elliot and Lisa Hogg was to use a number of financial stepping stones to reach the end of the season. Mostly the finance would come from the SPL, but the league chiefs would only provide the money if Elliot could guarantee that the club would fulfil its fixtures. In turn, Elliot would only be able to guarantee the fixtures if the SPL would guarantee the money. It became a game of brinksmanship. The league did not want Gretna to go bust; not out of any sympathy for the club – they just didn't want the embarrassment and the hassle. Elliot also wanted to keep Gretna going – if the club reached the end of the season intact, there was more chance of it being bought by another party, more of the creditors being paid, and, of course, for Wilson Field; this was another job, for which the company would be paid.

There was one other big stepping stone – the potential money-spinner of a home game against Celtic on Sunday 23 March. This game was due to be televised and would be worth somewhere between £100,000 and £150,000 for the club.

For the game before that, away to Aberdeen on Saturday 15 March, six of the players decided not to travel, having been given no promises about wages or insurance. At least one of the tabloids took advantage, sending a group of partially clothed young women to stand in the cold outside the ground with buckets for donations. There was help from other unexpected quarters too. An Aberdeen restaurant, The Crocket Hat, sent free meals to the Gretna players for after the game and a £500 donation was received from the supporters of Third Lanark, the last Scottish club to have been liquidated in 1967. It was also reported that a Gretna supporter called Malcolm Dunn had personally paid for the team coach to make the trip.

A few hundred miles south in Dumfries, as the half-time scores from around the country were being read out, the old rivalry at Queen of the South was too strong to allow any sympathy. 'Aberdeen 1, what's left of Gretna 0,' was heard from the tannoy and greeted with some amusement. Up at Pittodrie, Gretna's weakened squad could not prevent a further two goals: final score Aberdeen 3, Gretna 0. Worse was to come. On the bus home, the Gretna team heard the news that Motherwell had taken the decision to close Fir Park for the foreseeable future. It was not an attempt to upset Gretna – in fact Motherwell had responded to Gretna's crisis helpfully by offering to renegotiate the terms of the rent agreement. It was, the apologetic chairman stated, the only option left to fix the underwater drainage problems at the ground.

Whatever the reason, it now meant that Gretna's lucrative match with Celtic the following week was in danger. Celtic offered to stage it at their ground, but the proposal was rejected by the SPL. Hampden was touted as a possible alternative, a venue close enough to the tens of thousands of Celtic fans for Gretna to be happy with it, but instead the incomprehensible choice of Livingston was made, adding another thirty miles each way for both sets of fans. Well, at least the game was still on.

A deal was finally reached between Elliot and the SPL on Thursday 20 March which meant that some of the uncertainty disappeared. Cash would be provided to cover the players' wages (including back pay) and ensure that Gretna would be able to play all of their remaining games. Meanwhile, the outcome of the meeting with Roddy Collins was awaited, while Paul Davies had yet to hold talks with Elliot. A further consortium, American-based, was also said to be interested in the club.

On Easter Sunday, the attendance at Gretna's home game against Celtic, played 100 miles from Raydale, nearer Edinburgh than Glasgow, was a paltry 3,651. Hundreds of other fans had travelled but were turned away and told that the game was all-ticket. Despite the situation, no one was allowed to pay at the gate, a decision that was beyond the control of the administrator. It was criticised by Mick Wadsworth, who knew that every extra £10 would help. The big payday was a flop. As for the game itself, Gretna lost 3-0, despite a spirited performance from Greg Fleming in goal. Any mathematical hopes that Gretna might escape relegation were quashed the following week with a 2-0 defeat from St Mirren. By that stage, no one was particularly interested in the results. The main concern was the survival of the 62-year-old football club.

10

During the last week of March, with Gretna's players given dispensation from FIFA to sign for other clubs outside of the transfer window until the end of the month, the exodus began. The French duo, Aurelien Collin and Mickael Buscher, were the first to leave. All the talk of extending Fabian Yantorno's contract was shown to be ridiculous when the club let him go, protesting that it could not afford to pay for his rehabilitation. The Uruguayan had not played since being injured in a clash with the Falkirk goalkeeper on 19 January.

Despite assurances of cash from the SPL, David Elliot and Lisa Hogg knew they still had to cut costs. The league money would pay some of the bills but could not cover all of the ongoing expenditure, so on Wednesday 26 March they handed redundancy notices to twenty-nine staff. This included thirteen youth players, six community coaches and nine senior players. The latter bunch consisted of, in addition to Collin and Buscher, Henry Makinwa, David Mathieson, Chris Innes, David Bingham, Mark Birch, Erik Paartalu and Michael Tait. European scout Ray Farningham also lost his job. At the top of the club, Graeme Muir had already resigned and now that Brooks Mileson was, according to the administrator, 'no longer putting forward funds to allow the club to continue,' there was no need to keep Craig Mileson on the club's payroll. The timing was harsh for the senior players; although they had until the end of the month to register for other clubs, the English system meant that if they wanted to move south of the border they had only until 27 March, less than twenty-four hours, to do that. However, for others at the club, those with a much lesser public profile, the youth players and coaches, the situation was even harsher and the opportunities less obvious.

On Thursday 27 March, the Gretna Supporters' Society held an open meeting in the social club. Pete and I decided to go along and offer any support we could. My nine-year-old son, Rufus, sat beside us.

The meeting was chaired by the GSS Chairman, Craig Williamson, a lifelong resident of the town and owner of CSW Insurance, his office just around the corner from Raydale. He had also once played for the club. Also at the top table were Ron MacGregor and James Proctor from Supporters Direct Scotland.

The 200 or so who attended the meeting listened and talked for two hours while discussing how they could help to save the current club and work with the new owner should there be one. Ron MacGregor updated the supporters on the latest position with the administrators: there was one strong candidate looking to buy the club, but the outcome depended on the amount of money involved and what league Gretna FC would be in next season. James Proctor summarised similar experiences at other clubs; a Raith Rovers fan, he had helped to organise sponsored walks and other fundraising events. Williamson suggested that the supporters' society should set up an action group principally to lead on raising money.

As well as the supporters, another group of residents attended the meeting. This group, who would later call themselves the Fighting 46, were more concerned with what would happen to the social club and the Sunday market should Raydale be sold. They claimed that Raydale could not be sold because it did not properly belong to Gretna FC. Mileson, they said, had effectively stolen the land and therefore the administrator had no rights over it. At the meeting, their statement was the cue for a release of some long-held resentment against the Mileson family. Far from being a community club, they had in fact driven the locals out, using Gretna for their own celebrity-seeking ambitions and had now walked away from it, leaving it crippled, if not fatally wounded.

At this point, somewhat to my surprise, I noticed that Rufus had stuck his hand up in the air. When he began to talk quietly into the microphone, others in the crowd continued their discussions about who was to blame for the crisis. Aware that Rufus was not getting a fair hearing, Craig Williamson asked the nine-year-old to come to the front of the audience. He calmly delivered a short speech about how we should stop arguing about what had happened and that we should be looking to the future, either to help the club survive or by forming a new club. He had some ideas about fundraising, such as a family fun day, and those were the sort of things we should be talking about.

I do not want to exaggerate the effect on the meeting. It wasn't a piece of sentimental oratory, but it did at least bring the topic back to what we should do now rather than seeking blame for where we were. And it certainly worked on me.

At the end of the meeting, we approached the top table and Craig congratulated Rufus on his contribution. 'Dad,' he suggested, 'you should volunteer for the action group.' So I did, as did Pete. Craig said he would be in touch.

With Gretna's relegation confirmed the following Saturday at St Mirren, talk across the country turned again to the question of the club's long-term prospects. Davie Irons was struggling with his new job in the First Division and was deep in the turmoil of a relegation battle. He told the BBC that even if Morton avoided the drop, he did not expect to be facing his old club next season: 'I don't think they will survive.' As for Mileson's apparent refusal to help his once-beloved club: 'I still don't think that Brooks would walk away from Gretna. His illness must be so bad that he can't do anything about the situation, otherwise it is bizarre.'

On 1 April, as I was travelling back by train from London after a work-related trip, my mobile rang. It was Craig Williamson inviting me to a meeting the following Thursday to discuss the next steps for the new action group. Paul Davies, the agent who wanted to buy the club and the son of Gretna's head of security, would be there to outline his plans for the club. Craig asked if I would ring Pete and ask him along too. Mobile signals being what they are on trains, I realised that I was shouting through the handset at Pete and repeating things two or three times. Having eventually got the message through, I put my phone away, realising that half a dozen or so other people were looking at me, no doubt wondering why on earth I had been talking, loudly and repetitively, about some guy who was hoping to buy a football club. Pete had been able to tell me during the conversation that, according to the news, the administrator had set an asking price of £800,000 for the club.

A couple of days later, the action group meeting was held in the Richard Greenhow Community Centre in Gretna. There were around thirty in attendance, as well as Paul and Ken Davies. James Proctor from Supporters Direct came along again, bringing Elaine Millar with him, and emphasised the importance of a campaigning committee to keep up local and national interest. It would also be useful, he noted, to lobby local councillors, MSPs and MPs.

Ken Davies had done some homework and brought along a list of things that needed to be done to get Raydale fit for First Division football. The meeting was told that Paul, his son, was close to finalising an offer to buy the club. However, Paul's offer was dependent on Gretna being no lower than the First Division next season and most people were already aware that the Scottish Football League was unhappy with the general state of Raydale. The improvements would cost £35,000 and it was agreed that figure would be the first target for the action group. It felt both achievable and tangible; the money would be used for something which would be apparent to the supporters, rather than disappearing into wages.

At the meeting, as well as Craig and James, there were a handful of prominent contributors. One of these was a large, soft-spoken, articulate chap with the name of Malcolm Dunn. Malcolm lived in Windermere where he ran a mortgage advisory business. As well as well as being a passionate and well-connected Manchester United fan, he had been making the trip to Raydale frequently in recent years. Malcolm had been the supporter who had personally paid for the team coach to travel up to the Aberdeen game on 15 March when it looked like it might not take place.

Tony Woffindin was one of the most committed long-distance Gretna fans. He hailed from Chorley in Lancashire and was well known on the message boards as 'Chorley Tony', taking endless stick from Queen of the South and Carlisle United fans in particular for being a glory hunter who had only started coming to Raydale and Fir Park once the club had become successful. To be fair to Tony, this was something he never denied – he hadn't really heard about Gretna until they started to become something of a sensation – yet this was no reason to criticise him with such vehemence. In defiance, Tony continued to support the club, making journeys with his wife Jani of over 200 miles each Saturday, their singing loud enough to be heard above the taunts of opposition supporters. Tony worked in IT and was happy to offer his assistance.

By the end of the evening, Malcolm had been elected chairman of the action group, I was secretary, Tony would help Steve English with the website. Pete would be treasurer, supported by fellow accountant John Bowdon. Another supporter, David Mackie, who had previously been involved in fundraising and talking with the media for Gretna Supporters' Society, agreed to help out and be part of what was being called the action group sub-committee. The smaller group agreed to meet the following Monday at the Solway Lodge hotel bar in the town along with other members of the supporters' society board.

At the weekend, Gretna lost their home league game 2-1 to Inverness Caledonian Thistle and once again broke their own record of lowest SPL attendance. This time only 431 spectators paid to watch the game. Meanwhile, Edinburgh-based East of Scotland League club Spartans were publicly denying plans to take over the club from the border, in much the same way as Airdrie United had done with Clydebank. 'We have had very, very informal talks with the Gretna administrators, the SFL and SPL,' admitted their general manager, Derick Rodier, but it looked more likely they would be joining the small group of clubs waiting to submit an application should Gretna go bust.

On Monday 7 April, the action group met in the bar of the Solway Lodge, some of us clutching copies of the *News and Star* which reported that ex-Queen of the South manager Ian Scott was the latest name to be linked as the club's saviour, this time backed by a 'mega-bucks Californian business consortium' with £300 million available. At the meeting, Ken Davies gave us an update on the latest situation with his son's plans. Paul would be looking for the supporters or other investors to put around £300,000 into the club by buying shares. This would consist of individuals and groups who were in a position to put a significant amount into the deal, one of which could be the trust (on behalf of its members), and smaller investments from fans. Our view was that while this was worth pursuing, such a large figure might scare off some of the fans and therefore we decided to stick with a target similar to the one we had agreed the week before, £35,000, which would be linked specifically to ground improvements and getting Raydale up to First Division standard. The possibility of starting anew also hung over the group, so any funds raised could be helpful for that too.

On Wednesday 9 April, Gretna drew 0-0 at home with St Mirren. After the game, I finalised the first draft of a newsletter to send to fans. Craig had arranged for the database of society members to be sent to me, while Pete had pulled together the list of fundraising ideas – around fifty or so fans had submitted ideas to the supporters' society, ranging from raffles and collections to charity football matches and social events. The interest from Gretna fans, other clubs' fans and the press was, we reckoned, already at its peak and would wane as time went on. We had to make the most of it as soon as possible.

Tony had also been sent away to investigate the possibility of getting hold of some floodlights. Those at Raydale were technically not compliant with Scottish League standards, but Tony had been made aware that his local team, Chorley, had been donated some second-hand lights from Manchester United, but that Chorley were not able to use them. In the end his quest was fruitless, but it was an illustration of what we were prepared to consider. We also asked Craig to contact the club about the possibility of the supporters' society producing a matchday programme, which he did in between running his business and keeping track of the other group which arranged a separate public meeting 'to discuss the future of Gretna Football Club and Raydale Park'.

The force behind this group, the Fighting 46 (referring to the year in which Gretna FC had been formed), was a retired schoolteacher who now had a permanent stall on the market, Grace Hind. Grace had been involved in the old supporters' club but had decided not to be involved with the supporters' society. Her main grievance dated back to the original purchase of the ground in 1946. It had, she said, been purchased 'by four businessmen who then gave it to the community for the purpose of playing football', but it had never actually been owned by the football club. Therefore any subsequent transfer when Mileson became involved was not legally valid. It could not be sold by the administrator and could not be part of any deal involving any potential new buyers.

The point had been made at the original open meeting at the social club in March and was supported by a number of Gretna residents. Craig went to see Grace at her house in the town and tried to make the obvious point that no one would buy a football club without its home ground, but his pleas for all fans to work together seemed to fall on deaf ears.

By the time of Gretna's next game (Saturday 19 April, a 0-0 draw at Falkirk), there had been a number of developments. There was good news for some of the players who had been dismissed. Fabian Yantorno had been offered the chance to recover from his injuries at Hibernian while Chris Innes, having missed the deadline for playing in the UK, seemed set to follow Kenny Deuchar across the Atlantic after being offered a trial at New York Red Bulls.

At the action group we had also finalised our first newsletter and it had been emailed and posted out to the

450 names on the supporters' society database. In it we very deliberately set out our stall:

> Gretna FC is <u>not</u>, we feel, about poaching supporters from elsewhere or trying to outdo other clubs in the area. We are a small club and always will be. And first and foremost we are a community club. However that should not stop others from joining us and helping us along the uncertain journey we have in the near future. Statistically it has been said that we are the best supported club in the country (with crowds of more than 50% of our catchment), but we are not interested in statistics. We are only interested in ensuring that there continues to be football in Gretna and to rekindle the fantastic community work which this club has undertaken in the past.

We also confirmed that we had been speaking with 'a prospective buyer' (Paul Davies) and that we had set an initial target of £35,000 which would be used 'to improve Raydale and make it fit for First Division football'. The plan was for this to increase in order to 'enable supporters and the community to have a bigger say' in the way the club would be run. The subtitle of the newsletter was 'Rebuilding for the Future'.

I contacted Amanda Little at the *News and Star* and various other local and national media and this led to an article on 16 April where Malcolm confirmed that Gretna Supporters' Society was supporting Paul Davies' bid, and a promise from the newspaper of a more in-depth piece about the action group in the near future.

Malcolm attended the Fighting 46 meeting which had been held midweek. He took with him John and Sandra Bowdon who handed out copies of the newsletter. Over 100 people had turned up and, while interested in Grace's arguments that Raydale should never have become part of Gretna FC in 2004, they were less impressed with the predictions that a legal fight might cost £250,000.

Meanwhile, plans for what we hoped would be our major fundraising event, a 'Black and White' evening gala with auction, were being developed. Chief organiser was Jani Woffindin, Chorley Tony's wife, while others set about trying to obtain items for the auction. Craig started the list by handing over a football signed by the Ross County squad after that momentous final day match the previous year.

In the newsletter, we asked if supporters thought we should ditch the 'Living the Dream' motto which had frankly become a bit embarrassing. Suggestions for a replacement started to come in and while most were an improvement, we soon decided that the team could survive without a slogan. What was interesting was the geographical spread of support for the club, bringing good wishes and occasionally some much-welcome cash. There were greetings from fans who lived in London who, having never ventured north, had decided to make Gretna their second team, sending the occasional donation and watching for their results at teatime on Saturdays. Elsewhere in the UK, we sent the newsletter to places as far apart as Aberdeen and Devon, Manchester and Kent.

Internationally, Germany was well represented with fans from Berlin, Flensburg and Wildeshaven. The farthest fan hailed from Ontario, Canada.

Press interest increased. Katherine Elliot, a fan of the club, was also a reporter with the *Annandale Observer* and her offer to come and help out was quickly and gratefully accepted. Pete and I met up with ITV who wanted to do an interview to be broadcast locally. The incident which sparked the media attention was the publication that week of a list of people and firms owed money by Gretna.

The total debt came to £3.7 million. Over half of this was money owed to Mileson. The amount shown as owing to Heartshape, £1,871,428, was much lower than the sum which had been reported in the last set of accounts, £4,950,000. The next largest category was 'football debt'. Around £75,000 was owed to other clubs (mainly Motherwell), but this was dwarfed by the £800,000 claimed by Rowan Alexander. Unexpectedly, there was no such claim from Davie Irons. Martin Canning and James Grady were also shown on the list, owed £20,000 and £9,000 respectively.

The most important debt, for the survival of the club in any case, was £576,055 which was due to HM Customs and Excise and the Inland Revenue (although these had actually merged in 2005 to become HM Revenue and Customs). Of the 139 creditors, over 100 were local and often small companies owed anything between £20 and £75,000. Much hilarity was evident in the reporting that the latest instalment of the club's TV licence had not been paid. Even excluding the debt to Mileson's company, the remaining £1.9 million easily exceeded the valuation placed on the club's assets – principally Raydale, despite what Grace Hind and her Fighting 46ers argued – of only £824,000.

As well as the outstanding debt, there was also the money required to keep the club afloat, at least until the end of the season. Although the SPL had forwarded a cash advance of £272,000, this had effectively gone straight into the pocket of the administrator who, by charging £206 per hour, had made over £250,000 in the five weeks since being called in. Nevertheless, the administrator notified the last remaining director of the club, Ron MacGregor, that he had instructed chartered surveyors to begin preparing the sale of the ground.

After watching our first TV interview, I turned on my computer to find an email from 'a group of Norwegian investors' who were apparently in discussions to purchase Gretna FC. Their immediate plan was to ensure the safety of the club, while longer term they sought a return to the Premier League within three to four years and the development of a new 7,000 to 10,000 all-seater stadium at Raydale. To do this, the message read, they would need to have a close relationship with the club's sponsors and wanted some facts about how we were organised, how many of us there were. How would we feel about the club being taken over? Whilst our immediate response was to question the credibility of the query (were they really serious about a 10,000-seat Raydale?), we were careful not to be accused of ignoring any potential interest in the club and sent off a response which provided some facts about the society and said that we would be happy to have further discussions with them.

Meanwhile the 'old' Gretna, as we began to call them, seemed to be expiring, ironically with their best set of results since joining the Premier League. Three successive draws, against St Mirren, Falkirk and Kilmarnock, increased Gretna's points total by a third, bringing them back to the nine points they had originally had at Christmas. The Scottish Football League seemed to be acting sympathetically when it announced that following relegation, the club would be cleared to play in the First Division providing Raydale's much-needed improvements were carried out. Our £35,000 became even more important and the action group pulled together a diary of fundraising events which would take place over the following three months, including the Black and White Gala on 4 June and a sponsored walk in early July.

Inevitably there were tensions within the group. We were all volunteers, most of us with day jobs, some with families. More significantly, we were all complete novices at this sort of thing. Our main concern was to try and raise money to keep the 'old' Gretna alive, but deep down some of us had realised that we should be preparing to start all over again. Very rapidly, the remit of our action group was broadening, something with which not all members of the society were comfortable, although others understood it, indeed were desperate for us to pursue it.

I was also aware that the majority of those of us who were taking on a lot of the tasks were not from the town of Gretna itself – Pete and I lived within a few miles of each other to the east of Carlisle, Malcolm was from Windermere, John and Sandra hailed from further afield in Northumberland, and Tony and Jani from Chorley. It led to a few snappy comments about 'the outsiders', but I felt this could be remedied in good time. For the moment we simply had to make use of the willingness and skills of those who had volunteered to help, wherever they lived.

Our original intention had been for people to get on with implementing their ideas for raising funds. There would be some coordination, but as long as any idea raised money, no one should worry about seeking anyone's permission. In hindsight this was probably impractical and led to a mix up over whether signed shirts should be sold on eBay or kept for the gala auction. That marked the first falling out between members of the group; David Mackie resigned, albeit on friendly terms.

However we did realise the importance of controlling what we said to the media. In the early stages, a number of us spoke to the printed press, radio and television. Amanda Little from the *News and Star* asked to meet me to find out what we were up to and we arranged a date for 29 April. I was keen to ensure that the rest of the action group featured too, so the paper's photographer came to take some photos at our meeting the evening before. Amanda's article appeared the following weekend and mentioned how I had come to be involved in the campaign.

Beginning with 'nine-year-old Gretna fan Rufus Hodge knew what he had to do to help save his beloved club – he roped his dad into the fight for survival', the article picked up on our support for the Paul Davies bid but also helped to present the idea that, as I said, 'the bottom line is that we would like to see football being played in Gretna (next season). It might be non-league in either England or Scotland.' I also hoped that it could be an opportunity to repair old wounds: 'There are a lot of bridges to be built, especially if you look who is on the list of creditors.' I specifically mentioned the local council too, knowing that they would likely be the only ones able to take a decision about the future of Raydale.

We also heard back from the Norwegians. They said they were in touch with Paul Davies and were looking to coordinate their bid to buy the club with his. Revising their proposals for a new Raydale, they would also be looking to 'take an active ownership in the club by purchasing a shareholding and throwing all our experience and expertise into building a working business model for the club and to develop Raydale Park into a modern 5,000-7,000 capacity multi-purpose stadium, with the latest generation astroturf'. Once the club was profitable, they would look to sell their shareholding gradually to fans 'or other local interests, to ensure that the club stays in local ownership'.

This was more exciting and the information provided certainly appeared to be credible. The method they 'usually' followed (although, of greatest concern, we did not have any details of other clubs they had purchased, or indeed any references) was to buy a share of the club, use contacts and experience to develop it and then, over a five to ten year period, gradually sell the shares. They were now in the process of performing a 'due diligence' of the club's accounts and expected to be in Gretna soon. When they were, we could meet up and 'discuss how we can work together to ensure the dream continues', a phrase which, unknown to them, jarred a little.

Despite the lack of references, we were unwilling to rule anything out and I responded saying this was very encouraging and we would of course ensure that someone was available to meet them when they visited.

Back on the field, Gretna's mini-revival came to an abrupt halt with a 6-1 defeat at Inverness; the result, so late in the season, was the biggest league defeat the team had suffered. There now remained only two games. An away game at St Mirren was to be followed by a home game the following Tuesday. Exactly two years after the Scottish Cup Final, Gretna would again be playing Hearts.

Thanks to successful discussions between Craig Williamson and the club, we had been given two full pages of the matchday programme to use as we wished. We quickly prepared something which would again help to raise awareness of our efforts.

Before that, we were alerted by Ken Davies that news of our hard work had not yet penetrated the Scottish Football League and that questions were being asked by that august body as to whether anyone down there in Gretna really cared about what was happening. Whilst doubting the veracity of the information passed to Ken (we knew that the club had been in regular contact with the Scottish League, one result of which had been the league's reassurance about First Division status the following season), we nevertheless made sure that our primitive yet enthusiastic attention-seeking went into overdrive. Letters and emails were sent off to the league, to other clubs, to the national media in Glasgow and London, to the Scottish First Minister, the UK Prime Minister (who, like James Proctor from Supporters Direct, was a Raith Rovers-supporting Scot) and local MPs and MSPs. The politicians responded as politicians do, with soft messages of encouragement, but the Scottish League did not acknowledge the pack of data we sent to it.

The leak of information from the Scottish League also made us aware that (as we had expected for some time) while there was 'some support for Gretna FC ... There is strong opposition against [Gretna] on the management committee and other members of the league.' This was partly down to 'false promises of stadium development', but it was also undoubtedly the result of the arrogance of the club which had been seen in the previous few years and the open disdain shown by its owner to the Scottish footballing establishment.

The planned Norwegian visit did not materialise (they were 'stuck in Spain at the moment, in the middle of finishing negotiations on the purchase of a club here') but we organised a phone call to take place on Thursday 8 May, just before a small group was due to meet the administrator. During that phone call, the Norwegian Managing Director confirmed that a joint bid with Paul Davies was being worked up. Paul would put in 51%, the Norwegians 49%. Raydale would be redeveloped (with artificial turf: grass was apparently a 'huge waste of money') and then the Norwegians would sell back shares over twenty years. Their ultimate aim was to make a profit, and everything they had seen so far suggested that they were confident that Gretna FC could be profitable.

Craig, Pete and I then met administrators David Elliot and Lisa Hogg, who confirmed what they had earlier told a meeting of the creditors: that they knew of four potential bids, one of which was the proposed joint Davies/Norwegian submission. The deadline for all offers was Monday 19 May and if none was forthcoming then they would sell the assets (valued now at £874,000) to help repay the creditors. A creditors committee with a membership of five had been formed at the earlier meeting, and on it was our own Malcolm Dunn and also a local businessman who, we knew, was sympathetic towards the club. Two of the three others were, according to Elliot, 'hostile.' These were the architect who had drawn up plans for the new Raydale and proposed Eco-stadium, owed around £23,500, and HMRC. The fifth member was the SPL who, we suspected, would have very little interest in the club once the season had ended.

Rowan Alexander had unexpectedly turned up at the meeting. Ironically the man who had done so much for Gretna was now one of the biggest hindrances to its survival. If his £800,000 claim was defined as a football debt, its size would be a barrier to any future owner. Other claims from recent players were also being talked about, notably from David Bingham and Ryan Baldacchino. To end that rather strange day, as I drove home from the meeting with Elliot and Hogg I was bemused to hear Radio Cumbria report that Raydale belonged to 'the citizens of Gretna' and not to the football club.

Amidst all of this, there were still two games of football remaining. On Saturday 10 May, Gretna recovered from the previous week's mauling to draw 0-0 at St Mirren, the young Black and White team taunted mercilessly by the Paisley fans.

We had prepared well for the final game of the season, knowing that it might be Gretna's last. Our two pages in the programme sought to capture the history of the club by featuring two of the longest-serving supporters, Morag Wood and Margaret Robinson. Both had been involved in the club for a very long time – as a five-year-old Morag had been given the job of taking the oranges out to the players at half-time back in the 1950s. Switching to the younger fan base, we also used a piece that Rufus had written detailing the excitement of the trips to Hampden and Dingwall, ending with a plea to help the club survive.

Our message, we hoped, was clear: this club has been around for some time and in recent times we have seen a fair bit of excitement for young and old. Don't let it die.

The entire remaining squad of nineteen players, both youngsters and the more experienced, was listed on the back page, in stark contrast with the thirty-two from Hearts. Inside, a diary of the season read like a Sophoclean tragedy. The final outcome seemed so obvious in hindsight, yet was still nervously awaited. A special feature on 'veteran' Gavin Skelton, who was still only twenty-seven, prepared the fans for a special award to be presented to him before the game.

It was a fitting memorial for the club but by the time we arrived at Fir Park, all copies of the final Gretna FC programme had been sold out. We watched helplessly as a couple of opportunists lifted piles of them into a car and sped off, away from angry Gretna fans and towards their computer screens and eBay. Fortunately, the club had enough life left in it to ensure that more copies were printed and the real fans would eventually get their hands on the macabre souvenir.

As for the game itself? For ninety minutes it was scrappy. Hearts' Gary Glen was sent off after twenty-five minutes for kicking out at Craig Barr, while Rostyn Griffiths seemed to have put Gretna ahead just before half-time, only to be ruled offside. Then it all ended just as it should have. In the last seconds, Gavin Skelton picked up the ball about fifteen yards from the Hearts goal and slotted it calmly into the net. We celebrated as if Gretna had just won the Third Division, the Second Division and the First Division all over again; as if we'd actually won that Scottish Cup Final and done better in Europe; as if we'd held on in that game the previous November against Celtic or Kenny Deuchar had scored one more against Rangers in his last ever game for the club; as if Gretna FC was not going to die.

Rowan Alexander was at the game, sitting in the comfort reserved for directors and club officials. At half-time I took the opportunity to approach him. He looked a bit anxious when I approached, but relaxed when I thrust a fundraising leaflet into his hand. I intended to say something good to him, I don't know what, perhaps praise him for what he had achieved with the club, but then ask him to help out by dropping, or at least reducing, his ridiculous claim for £800,000. But when he looked up at me, I saw a man grieving, a man much more emotionally drained than I was. All I could say was 'help us'. I think he misunderstood, perhaps seeing it as a request to come back, because he smiled, the sadness gone for an instant.

In the next few days there were rumours and counter-rumours about potential buyers. I gave an interview to the *Independent on Sunday*, who seemed more interested in persuading me to lay blame at the Mileson family than on what we were trying to do with the supporters' society, and another to the *News and Star* in which, remaining optimistic, I expressed certainty that a bid would be tabled before the administrator's deadline crashed into us the following weekend.

In the end, the deadline came and went without any offer being made, but Paul Davies did contact David Elliot to confirm that one would be forthcoming shortly. The administrator granted a temporary stay of execution. Although he felt he had to send redundancy notices to all remaining staff at the club, no winding up order was made while discussions continued.

Davies' bid was dependent on the club playing in the First Division the following season. A team at that level, he believed, could generate enough income and continued interest to justify the cash he and the Norwegians would inject, along with funds from the supporters. Everything therefore relied on the Scottish Football League not relegating Gretna further down the league, but a positive decision for Gretna needed a robust business plan from Davies – but he needed a positive decision for Gretna before he could fully commit.

The signs were not hopeful. A separate bid, led by ex-youth coach Iain Scott, had floundered over what Scott described as rigid financial conditions. 'Personally I don't think there's a hope the club will survive,' he said. 'I think if [they do] it will be in the Scottish Third Division, which is very sad.'

The next steps were for David Elliot to have a look over Davies' offer and plans, and then give his view of it to the Scottish League. He would also ask the five members of the creditors committee to approve it, which they did on Thursday 22 May. Now all that was required was SFL blessing.

As Malcolm Dunn was in Moscow watching Manchester United beat Chelsea on penalties in the Champions League Final, Ron MacGregor attended on his behalf.

On Thursday 29 May, Ron once again travelled to Hampden to argue the case for Gretna's membership of the Scottish Football League. Six years before, the situation had been very different. Then he had, after some years of preparation, been bringing a well-developed case to admit a small but essentially sound team back to its homeland. It was a homecoming for a team that had done itself proud across the border as representatives of one of the most famous wee towns in Scotland.

This time Ron, the last representative of that club, was swimming against a tidal wave or recrimination, uncertainty and the spiteful froth of *schadenfreude*. The committee had been impressed by Gretna's case in 2002, seeing it as honest and full of integrity – especially when compared with the distaste held by some about the newly formed Airdrie United. In 2008, some of that committee, after years of watching with disbelief, envy and embarrassment as Gretna rose and rose, had now become inclined to teach the small club from the border an unforgettable lesson. The problem was that in doing so they would also be killing off any last chance of the club's survival. They were no more responsible for Gretna's spectacular demise as they were for the club's earlier success. Nevertheless, the chairmen knew that if they chose not to show compassion to the club, Gretna FC would finally slip away. The committee consisted of Brown McMaster (Partick

Thistle), Jim Ballantyne (Airdrie United), Vivien Kyles, (Livingstone), Euan Cameron (Alloa), Gordon McDougall (Cowdenbeath), Alan Ripley (Arbroath), Donnie MacIntyre (Dumbarton) and Les Gray (Hamilton). Ballantyne was not permitted to vote – not because of any historical friction dating back to 2002, but because should Gretna be relegated to the Third Division, Airdrie would be promoted to the First, despite losing the play-off final to Ayr United. In a similar way, Stranraer would achieve promotion to the Second Division.

Just in time for the meeting, Brooks Mileson finally spoke up. Or rather, a note was presented to the committee from the still ill businessman which stated that he would be willing to transfer his shares to Davies. What impression this made on the meeting is hard to measure but, if anything, it seemed to stiffen attitudes. At first, some harsh financial conditions were imposed. A £200,000 bond was to be paid 'up front'. A new stand had to be built to segregate home and away supporters, costing at least another £100,000, and any outstanding football debt would have to be cleared. Then, asking Elliot if he could guarantee that the rescued club would be able to fulfil its fixtures the next season, the administrator, his professional judgement on the line, felt unable to say yes. The Scottish Football League representatives then, in the full knowledge that Paul Davies' bid would be withdrawn should they relegate the club to the Third Division, did exactly that.

That evening, the action group met with heavy hearts. Paul Davies attended and confirmed that his bid was now in tatters. We had little choice but to accept his decision. At least we knew that now we had to prepare for a new club, although we realised that it would now become much more difficult to raise funds.

Our attempts had made disappointingly slow progress. With only £1,600 collected so far, our target of £35,000 now seemed impossible. There were also grumbles about lack of interest in some of the planned events. A Body Shop party attracted only five attendees (although it clashed with that Champions League final), but we still had our two largest dates to come: a sponsored walk on Sunday 6 July, organised by John and Sandra, and the Black and White Gala due to take place on 4 June. Ticket sales for the latter had also been slow and were not helped when the initially promised attendance of some of the (now ex-) players failed to come good.

Nevertheless, we now had confirmation that what we should be concentrating our efforts on was a brand new club in the town: a successor to the old Gretna FC (which would now formally cease to exist), but in many ways returning to the original premise of that club. When people thought about Gretna, most linked the club solely with the past five years: the Mileson era with its promotions, trophies, records and headlines. That was understandable, very few outside the community were aware of the history prior to that time. Over the next few weeks we told anyone who listened that we were building a new club which was going to be very different from the old one. What we really meant was that it would not be like Mileson's Gretna: it would be Gretna's Gretna once again.

11

How do you found a football club?

We set up a small group – Helen and Ron MacGregor, Pete George and myself – to do three main things. The first was to talk with the administrator and clarify the Raydale issues. The second was to raise the profile of the new club, even before it existed, and to talk with local politicians. The third, most importantly, was to try and find out how on earth someone went about the business of setting up a brand new senior football club!

Our questions about Raydale focused very much on finding out the administrator's intentions. During phone calls over the following days, he explained that it was still his plan to sell the ground but, while it remained in his hands, he would be willing to consider any proposals for its use. He said he was aware of the Fighting 46 group and their claims over land ownership but as he had not received anything in writing from them he could not discuss it further.

I also spoke with the company whom Elliot had commissioned to take care of the disposal of assets, Eddisons of Sheffield. They confirmed they had no problem with the supporters' society being handed the remaining merchandise from the club shop. This would be a useful addition to our fundraising stock.

I then called Grace Hind from Fighting 46, asking her to consider that we should be working together to persuade the administrator that Raydale continue to be used for football. Grace was polite but would not commit to any agreement. She also questioned Elliot's claim about lack of contact from her group, so I now wasn't sure who was telling the truth.

On Saturday 31 May, Pete, Rufus and I began our new publicity push in person by setting up a stall at Gretna Gateway, a large discount shopping centre on the edge of town which pulled in a vast number of visitors as they travelled across the border. We collected £110 and were more heartened that most of those who stopped for a chat had heard what we were up to. In the next few days, I managed to do a number of media interviews: BBC Scotland, ITN, the Press Association and Radio 4's PM show. It was all a little surreal, the latter in particular, sitting alone in a studio at BBC Radio Cumbria waiting to be connected live to Eddie Mair, who hosted the national teatime news show. I had visited the studios in Carlisle before, when promoting my previous books, and always found the staff to be friendly. This time, with a link to the PM show, I was treated like a VIP!

We also agreed a set of key principles for the action group to use if being interviewed, or just questioned, by the press. These served as useful reminders of where we had got to and where we thought we were heading. While we prepared for the birth of a new club, we continued to pay lip service to the possibility of the old Gretna some-how escaping death and were still hoping to work with another buyer if one came forward. On the other hand, a new club would be an entirely separate entity and not related to those who had been in charge in the past. The exception was the MacGregors, who were well respected throughout Scottish and English football, and who were helping us with their contacts and experience.

We would also be putting pressure on the administrator regarding the sale of Raydale. Whilst behind the scenes we all accepted that the Fighting 46 case was weak, we would opportunistically remind the media – and potential buy-ers of the ground who may not have been interested in acquisition for footballing purposes – of the questions hanging over the issue of ownership. Linked to this were the limitations placed on the ground by the council regarding anything other than sports or recreational use.

As for the Scottish League and others, we wanted to draw a line under what had happened in the past. 'Despite our anger with other clubs and the SFL,' I wrote, 'we are looking to build bridges. The main reason we are being kicked on the way down is because we are perceived to have trampled over others on the way up. So the new Gretna will build relationships with other clubs – we may need their support again one day.'

We chose not to comment on why things went wrong or play the blame game. There was to be no finger pointing. Finally, we promised that we would be holding a public meeting soon to discuss the future, assuming of course that there was support for a continuation of football in the town.

Although we were increasingly distancing ourselves from the fatally wounded club, we continued to push for some of the old players to attend the Black and White Gala. As part of this, Jani Woffindin also spoke to Rowan Alexander, an interesting conversation in which the ex-manager and one-time Gretna hero gave his view that a Third Division Gretna was the best option. The revamped club could resume its community work and rebuild from the bottom. The flaw in this plan was that it would still need a cash injection along the lines that had been proposed by Paul Davies and the Norwegians, except they had required First Division status.

Others were also getting in touch. I had a friendly email from the Norwegians expressing their sorrow that 'the deal we were proposing with Paul Davies did not go through', but also promising that they would help 'in any way we can to keep a football club going in Gretna, and once you have gotten somewhere with these plans, please contact me and we will help out as a sponsor for the club for the first couple of seasons or so'.

Simon Cope, the chairman of Scarborough Athletic FC (whose predecessor club, once owned by Mileson, had also gone bust), wrote to offer whatever support and advice he could. I arranged to meet him at the forthcoming Supporters Direct Conference in Stirling at which he would be speaking.

The next interesting correspondence to hit my inbox was an email from Alistair Barron, the architect owed money by Gretna FC and one of the members of the creditors committee. Rather than being the volley of hostility which might have been expected, Alistair's note was sympathetic and constructive, suggesting that we ask the administrator for ownership of the name 'Gretna Football Club' and making some suggestions about using Raydale while it was still in his possession. In the end, Barron was as much a victim as the supporters – even more so, given the £23,500 owed to him.

On the same day, a more intriguing message arrived. Someone called Jon Callaghan suggested copying the model which had enabled Ebbsfleet United FC to go from certain death to winning the FA Trophy. A website had been set up (MyFootballClub.co.uk) and fans who donated £35 could have a say on transfer and other major decisions, including the chance to offer tactical and team selection advice. Membership reached 27,278 and their cash earned them 75% of the club. We were dubious about Callaghan's idea, which he would run from his base in Poland, but as he had been involved with the club in the past we promised to keep in touch. In the end we did not take up the idea and felt vindicated to learn a couple of years later that it had not really solved Ebbsfleet's money problems.

On Tuesday 3 June, David Elliot tendered Gretna's resignation from the Scottish Football League, so ending a short six-year life during which Gretna played in all four of the Scottish divisions, winning three of them. The path was now cleared for other clubs to apply and four set about finalising their proposals: Spartans (the favourites), Cove Rangers, Preston Athletic and neighbours Annan Athletic.

Newspapers and other media were finally able to use their long-prepared obituaries, with *The Scotsman* pointing out that 'even if a new team arises from the ashes of the current club, the sale of Raydale would leave any reincarnation with nowhere to play'. Others simply put the boot in including – perhaps unsurprisingly – Geoff Brown, the St Johnstone chairman still apparently smarting from the failure of his eve of Dingwall public message. Open letters were written in the press asking Mileson to come out of hiding and make one last gesture to help the supporters set up a new club. Others who had benefited at Gretna in past times refused to take pot shots at Mileson. Steve Tosh was one of those, reserving his anger instead for Mick

Wadsworth and what he believed was the Yorkshireman's disrespect to Scottish players, teams and the leagues. 'He decided to get rid of players who were quite capable of playing at SPL level and replace them with young kids from England,' he said.

Little wonder that our supposed major fundraising gala, held the day after resignation from the Scottish Football League, felt more like a wake than a celebration. Fewer than fifty of the tickets had been sold, but nevertheless we dressed up and had what fun we could. The event did raise some money – £1,300 – although it was mainly just the same small group of people contributing, including Rufus who spent his savings on one of Kenny Deuchar's shirts. If nothing else it was an event at which we could let our hair down before what was expected to be a maelstrom of hard work. The next season started in two months' time. The race was on, not just to start a new club, but also to get a squad together, a manager, find somewhere to play and, most importantly, membership of a league.

On Sunday 8 June, the day after I had attended the Supporters Direct Conference in Stirling at which I received many messages of support and encouragement from other clubs, I was taking a break and enjoying the early summer warmth with the kids at Talkin Tarn, a small lake to the east of Carlisle, when my phone rang. It was then that I first heard the voice of Stuart Rome, the reserve coach at Workington Reds FC, a team then in the Conference North. Stuart's main job was Director of Football at Newton Rigg Campus, where Gretna FC's academy was hosted, but his connections with the club went back further. Now in his late forties, Stuart, a lifelong resident of Gretna, had once played for his hometown club and had been in the side which enjoyed the club's first ever FA Cup game on 3 September 1983. He had then gone on to be a youth coach with the club. An old friend of Ron and Helen MacGregor, he had been encouraged by them to ring me and offer his help.

The roots of a new football club began to take hold. Our main concerns – the areas in which we were lacking – could be summarised in four main questions: Who would manage the team? From where could we get some players? Where would we play, if not at Raydale? How could we join a league (and which league)?

Stuart had answers to all four. He was prepared to resign from Workington and become our first manager on a voluntary basis. He was currently working with around forty kids at the west Cumbrian club and Newton Rigg and could guarantee that he would bring a squad with him. If Raydale was not available, why not try the Everholm Stadium at Annan, previously used as a training facility by Gretna FC? It was in better condition than many of the grounds in either the South or East of Scotland Leagues – both of which, Stuart suggested, we should be applying to.

He agreed to come along to the action group meeting which had been scheduled for the following evening and also to our public meeting due later that week. Stuart listened very patiently as we went through some routine

ANTON HODGE

business. He was introduced to the group and he added that he was thinking of the longer term – a three-year plan through which he would bring his kids and turn them into a quality side. Local talent would also be mined, an aspect that found favour with those nurturing a desire to see the club become a community asset.

Stuart was good on detail: he had already looked at costs and explained to Pete his plan was certainly afford-able. Finally, in a move that was guaranteed to win over any remaining doubts, he passed around a catalogue of football strips containing an example of a strip with black and white hoops – old style, pre-Mileson. We agreed to his proposals in principle at the supporters' society board meeting held immediately after the action group, although a formal decision would be taken after Wednes-day's public meeting.

My presentation for that meeting was, thanks to Stuart's emergence, much more confident and substantial than it might otherwise have been. Press coverage was ris-ing, with the BBC, ITV and the *News and Star* all report-ing on the event. That same day, the Scottish Nationalist MSP Mike Russell issued a press statement arguing that the name of Gretna FC should be kept alive by 'upgrading Raydale Park into a multi-purpose sporting resource for the community'. In front of 120 or so attendees I reported on the work we had been undertaking and outlined the six aims and objectives we had for moving forward. These were:

1. To form a new club
2. To have a clear constitution
3. To play at Raydale
4. To play in the 2008-09 season (two months away!)
5. To re-establish strong community links
6. To be financially sustainable

As for the name of the new club, we decided to ask the schoolchildren of the area for suggestions. When the issue of the team's strip was brought up, there was overwhelming support for a return to the black and white hoops.

Discussions had already started with the South of Scotland League. Geographically this was the preference, albeit the quality was generally believed to be superior in the East of Scotland League. Although the aim to return to Raydale was largely a matter out of our hands, we would continue to have discussion with the council about any assistance they might bring to that purpose. Meanwhile, without explicitly mentioning the Everholm, I confirmed that we had a back-up plan which was being investigated. Stuart was introduced, although one attendee did suggest that the solution to our problems would be the return of Rowan Alexander.

The main message, and one that would remain important if the club were to return to the community, was that we needed local people to quickly become involved. 'We have to do something now,' I pleaded. 'We have weeks, not months.' With overwhelming support (and even an arm half-raised when the vote was called from the retired teacher heading Fighting 46), the board felt confident to meet straight away and agreed to appoint Stuart as manager. It was now all systems go, although the ex-Workington coach was just about to embark on his two-week summer holiday.

In his absence we continued with our work while press attention shifted to a public spat between Davie Irons and Mick Wadsworth over who was responsible for the old club's demise. Ron, Helen and I met Elaine Murray MSP in her Dumfries office. As politicians do, she offered some noises of encouragement but nothing really concrete, and I came away feeling that her heart wasn't really with us. This was not the case with all of her profession. Archie Dryburgh, a Dumfries and Galloway councillor, was a real driving force behind getting the council to consider the matter of Raydale, while at a national level, David Mundell MP was very supportive, sometimes taking the trouble to come along and support the team in those early games at the Everholm.

At the action group's next meeting on Monday 16 June, we planned our EGM, due to be held on the 7 July, and would seek the formal confirmation needed to establish the new club. I also updated everyone on discussions with the South of Scotland League and the Everholm situation. Dick Shaw was the secretary of the league and also held the same position at Annan Athletic. Ron and Helen, calling on years of friendship, had approached Dick about the possibility of joining the league and, in return, Dick had emailed the other clubs to canvass their views. Dick also set out some conditions such as access to a ground and a £300 bond. He mentioned that time was not on our side and that the league already had fourteen clubs, an even number. An odd number would be a drawback. Nevertheless, he agreed to get back in touch once he had heard from the others. The possibility of playing in the East of Scotland League looked less hopeful: there was apparently only one vacancy and three current applicants.

Everholm Stadium was owned by Annandale and Eskdale Leisure Trust, a former asset of the council which had been outsourced. Our main concern was that we needed to be able to guarantee its use at short notice, so it was decided that further discussions would be held with the managing director, Alan Barlow. Barlow, like most council officers I have come across, just wanted to help out. That proved instrumental in the end.

Stuart emailed from his holiday in the sun to say that Workington Reds had offered us the chance of a game on 12 July in Workington and would even pay our travel costs. He repeated his view that we should keep in touch with the East of Scotland League as backup. Mindful that news of his appointment would start to creep into the public domain, we put together a press release which also confirmed our application to the South of Scotland League. As with almost everything we did, there was the usual concern and criticism. From Cumbria there were accusations (to be fair, justified) from Workington fans about stealing the cream of their youth talent, while over the border there were some fairly harsh words about me being expressed on web message boards. The personal attacks did not really bother me, although I was worried that Rufus might somehow be dragged into or at least get to hear of it. My only worry was that the focus would shift away from the work we were doing and onto conspiracy theories about our motives. Pete and I, aided by Ron and Helen, were carrying out the bulk of the work. This looked a bit too much like outsiders plus the old guard for some. Mostly, it was simply an accident of timing. Craig Williamson was, like Stuart, Steve English and another key supporters' society board member, Doug Branney – all of whom were locals – on holiday during those important two weeks in June, though with the miracles of modern technology, we were all keeping in touch. There were others doing important work in the background, but the criticism seemed to arise from those who felt they should be involved but somehow never quite managed to offer more than a few anonymous suggestions on the internet about, for example, bringing Rowan Alexander back (in place of an 'unknown' Stuart Rome) and getting 'bums on seats' to fund our charge back to the Premier League.

In response to the criticism over Stuart's appointment, I reminded the snipers in the *News and Star* that we still didn't have a non-league place and repeated the request for volunteers to step forward. Nevertheless, I didn't know what to make of one rumour that I was Brooks Mileson's plant in the new club. Similarly, in a crowded late night train between Penrith and Carlisle, I didn't know whether to be amused or afraid when a group of swaying lads pointed me out as 'that football millionaire Miles Brookson'!

Pete's draft business plan, backed by about £4,000 in fundraising and put together with Stuart, estimated that a new club would have a turnover of around £14,000 per year. He continued to be in touch with the Norwegians who were now promising to pay for the club's new kit. Craig had also been back in touch on his return from holiday. Pete and I met up with him in the cafe of the kids' soft play area at Gretna Gateway. We must have looked odd, if not frankly suspicious, although my two sons were also there somewhere, letting off steam while we updated the Gretna Supporters' Society Chairman on events to date. Craig was grateful and supportive of our efforts and we agreed that we would all meet up with Stuart as soon as he was back.

The suggestions from the schoolchildren came back to us too – nearly 200 names were proffered – ranging from Gretna United to Blacksmith Rovers, from Border Lions and Gretna Tigers to the Border Busters and the Wedding Bells. Somehow 'Girly Football Club' also managed to sneak into the list. A shortlist was to be drawn up and presented to the EGM on 2 July.

As I had not heard from Dick Shaw, I emailed again on 25 June letting him know that our discussions with the leisure trust had gone well and we had secured the use of Everholm. Our long-term aim was to get back to Raydale and we were increasingly hopeful of achieving this – any purchaser would have to take note of the provision of the local plan which provides some safeguarding of the football pitch. I asked him for three things: an update on the other clubs' views and what else he needed from us, were the first two. The third was a sensitive one. We had been in communication with Carlisle United about possible use of the new enclosed training pitch and I asked Dick – stressing the confidentiality – for his views. Would such an arrangement make admission to the South of Scotland League more or less likely? In reality I was addressing the issue which I was beginning to think was a problem with the Secretary of Annan Athletic: would a Gretna team, playing at the Everholm in Annan, be a distraction for the town's own team, whose ground was just along the road from our proposed playing venue?

Dick's response was disappointing short, ignoring all of my questions: 'Mr. Hodge. I have issued the first batch of fixtures so any inclusion in the South of Scotland Football League this season would be very difficult. However I will keep clubs informed of your ongoing discussions.'

So on the 26 June I tried again, this time sending a two-page document headed 'Draft Application to join the South of Scotland League' and asking Dick to confirm if it was helpful. Although he had ignored my question about the views of other clubs, we knew from our own private contacts that they were generally supportive. We approached five of the fourteen and all indicated that they would welcome Gretna and its visiting fans to their grounds as a fellow league member. The next day, the *Annandale Observer* reported on a 'New Blow to Gretna', quoting Dick who claimed he had not received a formal application in time before the first fixtures were drawn up. This was true – the list had been put together some weeks before – but it did seem unhelpful timing for the unresponsive secretary to now publish the list while we were still in communication with him and seeking to be added to it. A further email to Dick on 30 June, again stating that the Everholm would be our playing venue, was met at first by silence then a letter in which Dick informed us that the executive committee of the league had met and decided not to consider our application further. 'Uncertainty over grounds issues' was quoted as the only reason, despite our assurances that there was no such uncertainty. As we then received information that at least two other members of the executive committee had not taken part in any such decision, I later wrote to Colin Holden, Chairman of the South of Scotland League. Why wasn't Dick responding to me? Who had taken the decision? Was there a potential conflict of interest, given Dick's very interesting comments that appeared in the *Sunday Mail* a few days later in which he claimed to take no pleasure in Gretna's downfall, but would nevertheless be trying to entice some of the club's fans away to support Annan? When the supporters' society board met on Monday 30 June, we agreed to approach the East of Scotland League. Stuart was tasked to do this, while we considered what, if any, options we had left with the South. Stuart's discussions proved far more encouraging than any of us believed and there was a possibility of appearing at an

EGM of the East of Scotland League on 10 July. The reason for calling that EGM was that the club which won the race to take the Scottish League place vacated by the old Gretna was one its members – Annan Athletic.

The news came through the day after our own EGM, which was held on 3 July. Our shortlist of five names (Gretna FC, AFC Gretna, Gretna United, Gretna Rovers and Gretna Athletic) was augmented by another suggestion, one which would commemorate the year of rebirth while continuing the history – Gretna FC 2008. A motion was passed to form a new, trust-owned club.

The vote was overwhelmingly supportive. The fans were fired up, as the supporters' society board and action group had been a few weeks earlier, by photos of the new kit. The actual result was 113 in favour, 1 against and 1 abstention. Gretna FC 2008 was born.

12

Our trip to the East of Scotland League EGM at Tyne-castle, the stadium of Hearts, was confirmed for Thursday 10 July, only two days before our first scheduled game at Workington. I began to prepare a speech which would hopefully persuade the committee to accept us as a new member. Craig, Stuart, Pete and I would travel to the nervy experience, all of us aware that refusal would probably ensure that our new club would effectively be stillborn. At our own EGM we were optimistic about gaining league status but admitted that a fall-back position would be to delay a year and have a season of friendlies. That prospect was unappealing. Surely our core fans would start to slip away if there was no competitive football in Gretna, perhaps driving the few miles along the A75 to Annan.

After weeks of media spotlight on those of us working on the administrative and governance arrangements of the new club, we began to push forward Stuart and some of the players who would be more interesting people to talk to the press. In his first major interview on the eve of our trip to the capital, Stuart highlighted those players who had won him the Lancashire League the previous season at Workington. Meanwhile, a little bit of light relief was had when the papers reported that East Fife's purchase of the new-ish Raydale South Stand had fallen through when the Second Division club realised that its roof was not part of the deal. In addition, the Fifers agreed with the administrator to buy some training goals, an ice maker and a chemical storage safe. When they sent someone to pick the items up, the driver (in the words of East Fife director Jim Stevenson), 'found a bunch of protesters who stood in the way as a blockade. We aren't going to put a driver in that position and we certainly wouldn't have asked him to cross a picket like that, so we just left it. And that was just a few bits – I don't know what it would be like if we tried to move a stand!'

The protesters were from Fighting 46, but the whole stand issue was further explained in an email from the administrator which stated that he had 'received strong interest from the council who appear to wish to acquire the whole site and allow football to continue in some form' and for that reason the main stand, plus any other equipment (goal posts, dugouts, etc) would not be leaving Raydale for the time being.

On the evening of Monday 7 July, Pete, Rufus and I got sight of our new players for the first time when we went to watch their training session in Carlisle. They were getting ready to do their job on the following Saturday. Before then – on Thursday at Tynecastle – we would have to do ours.

As Craig drove the four of us through the border hills and across towards the capital city, I read my prepared speech, wincing while delivering some of the more sentimental lines and wondering whether it might come across as too dramatic. The others did not seem to take it that way, although we were all perhaps too nervous to decide what was appropriate. On arrival, we saw the other club reps, most of whom had been telephoned by Stuart during the previous few days. His canvassing of opinions was the most important work that any of us had undertaken in the run up to the meeting and laid the groundwork for our success. However, as we waited in the corridor outside the room where the meeting was running through its initial business, all pacing back and forth, one or other of us visiting the toilet every few minutes, we had no idea how the other clubs really felt. Stuart's view was that the Borders clubs, especially Hawick and Selkirk, would be supportive. The reps from Dalbeattie Star also seemed to nod to us in agreement and we could only hope that the new boys from Stirling University would show the same grace as had been offered to them when their bid to join the league had been accepted only weeks earlier.

Eventually we were asked into the room. Stuart, Craig and Pete sat on three chairs at the front of the room and I stood up and cleared my throat. For the first few minutes I could hardly hear my own words and was genuinely concerned at the volume of my heart beating around 120 to the minute. I knew I had to keep it short and get to the points the clubs would need to hear about, but I also wanted to try and put the whole thing into context, to relay the fear and hopes that awaited their decision, 100 miles back down the road. I began by talking about the old and the new…

The old Gretna football club is practically finished. This ends sixty-two years of senior football in the town, mostly as a non-league side, but recently, as you will be aware, in the Scottish Football League and briefly the SPL. It is important to us not to forget the heritage of the club over six decades, where the club played an important role in the community and that is what we are trying to resurrect.

We are a new club – with a slightly different name from the old club – but there are some traditions we want to continue, and others we would rather forget about. This presents an opportunity, but also I know will cause you some concerns. You might ask us why you should even consider an application from a brand new club, with no accounts, not even a fully completed board. You will also I suspect have some concerns regarding where we will play. Over the next five minutes I hope to answer these concerns, but first will give you a little bit of background.

The supporters' trust – Gretna Supporters' Society – was formed in 2007, with the aim of giving fans more of a say in the running of what was then deemed to be a very successful club, at least on the playing field. We did not expect to be having to reform the club less than a year later, but that is where we are. Since the demise of the old club we have been working hard to do this, working with and receiving advice from other clubs in both Scotland and England, with Supporters Direct, the SFA, the various leagues. Some of you who have offered that advice are in this room and we are very grateful for it. We have held public meetings and EGMs of the trust, where we have received pretty much unanimous support for what we are doing. This has been exhausting for us – often being ridiculed by those who do not wish us to succeed.

Yet still we do it. Why?

The reason is very simple – we want the same thing that has led you into doing the jobs you do for your own clubs: we believe that football is a fantastic sport and we want to see it being played again in Gretna. And it's not just the winning or even the losing, or the no-score draw on a dreary day in January with the icy wind sweeping along the Solway shoreline. It's not just the heritage and the sixty-two years of history and the fact that all of that has been destroyed in the past few weeks.

It's also about the community work, working with the kids, getting involved in promoting the health and social inclusion agendas. This is what we will do, albeit at a pace which is more sustainable than last time.

It will be about watching a team put on a black-and-white hooped jersey and bringing families back to watch us, having fun and doing something worthwhile.

But I don't need to sell passion for the sport. You all have that too. I guess you are more interested in practical issues. So let's get straight to the issues.

Firstly, what is happening about Raydale Park? Well, the fact is that the administrator has put it up for sale, with a closing date for bids 24 July – two weeks today. We believe that one interested party is expected to put in an offer – Dumfries and Galloway Council, who will buy it for the community and allow the new club to play there.

There is a restriction on the use of the football pitch within the local plan, which will last until the end of 2009 and will almost certainly be renewed. This is, we know, putting potential purchasers off as it would restrict what they could do with over half of the land. However, potential buyers are being directed to us as we have said we will work with anyone who does buy it and negotiate renting it from them.

For this reason we have some confidence that we will be able to play at Raydale again, sooner rather than later. However, in the meantime, and for the purposes of this application, we have secured use of a pitch in Annan, seven miles away. This is an enclosed pitch with changing facilities and I have the written guarantee from the owners regarding use for home fixtures. We also have photographs which we can pass round.

I will be honest with you. We know from recent history about the mess which is caused when promises are made and not kept, so I will not do that. I will say that the pitch in Annan, the Everholm, is not ideal. It does, we feel, meet all the criteria you require, but we would be looking to move back to Raydale as soon as possible.

Secondly, what about lack of history? Well, again I will be honest with you. We are telling you that we are a new club, which we are, and although we will carry on some of the traditions, we do not have a history for you to see. All we can ask for is your understanding in this, just as other leagues have been understanding about clubs who have gone through the same as us and were allowed in within days of forming such as Scarborough, AFC Wimbledon, Airdrie United, Telford, the new club in Manchester, and other clubs who were allowed into leagues within a year of forming, such as Clydebank.

Our biggest danger is that nothing happens now, that we don't have a league to play in, that our players leave and that all the momentum and drive is lost. That is why we are asking your indulgence on this matter, while providing you with assurances on issues such as the ground and so on.

Thirdly, what about finance? We have copies of the business plan which we have put together which is realistic and the result of a lot of work and discussion with other teams. We have on the trust board, and expect to have on the football club board, a great deal of financial experience. Craig runs his own insurance business, both Pete and I are qualified accountants and are senior financial managers in local government. We will not allow the club to be financially unsustainable.

We have sponsorship arranged, kit, a manager and players. But we have also been raising funds too. In the past few months we have held a number of fundraising events and have funds available of over £20,000 to support the new club. We are prepared to pay over a bond to the League in lieu of our newness if that is required.

In conclusion, we hope that you will consider our case and will accept us into the League and we hope to be bringing a coach load of supporters to your grounds in the coming season. Mainly however, and more importantly, we hope to be seeing football once again in Gretna.

When I finished we trooped out, back into the corridor, not daring to look at each other, and waited.

And waited.

We could hear the conversation and discussion form the other side of the door, but frustratingly the words, punctuated (alarmingly) by regular explosions of laughter, were not clear enough to convey any meaning. Perhaps that was better in the end, not to be able to hear the debate, the vacillations, support, disagreements and counter-arguments. Stuart sat with his head in his hands. Over the course of the evening his recently acquired sun tan had paled, but now he burned more crimson with every passing minute. If they didn't tell us soon I honestly feared he would catch fire.

Still we waited.

Eventually it was Selkirk's chairman Jim Moody who emerged from the room and told us it was time. I am sure he smiled at me using only his eyes, his other features professionally and properly neutral. Stuart now looked close to collapse. As well as the expectations of the supporters, Stuart also had a whole potential squad of players awaiting his call.

The decision was to welcome Gretna FC 2008 into the East of Scotland League.

When it came it was almost too low key to be real. To the other club reps, this signalled that a bit of tidying up needed to be done with the fixtures and not much else. For us, the work required was immense. I felt like cheering, jumping up and down and shaking everyone's hand, but calmed down in time to hear the one condition placed on us – an inspection of the Everholm. That task was given to our neighbours from Dalbeattie Star and we felt confident there would be no problems there. We had done it!

The news travelled fast and on the way home I received a number of calls from journalists in Edinburgh, Glasgow, and the Borders. Stuart was busy ringing or sending messages to his squad, telling them to start preparing for the new club's first game – only two days away. By the time I got back home I was still buzzing, so I switched on the computer, poured a large celebratory whisky and started sending emails.

The next day I received an email from Annan Athletic – not from Dick Shaw, but from Neil Irving. This followed my note sent a week earlier which offered our congratulations to our neighbours in achieving Scottish League status. Neil expressed his best wishes to our new club – 'I think it is fantastic, the efforts made by yourself and fellow board members to re-establish a football club in Gretna' – and even mentioned the possibility of a pre-season friendly. It was important that the two clubs, who represented a combined footballing history of the neighbouring towns which reaches back over the decades, remained friends. I'm pleased to say, this has been the case.

On Saturday 12 July, Pete, Rufus and I travelled to the Sands Centre in Carlisle, where we were to be picked up by the team coach for the short trip down the west coast to Workington. We had also brought along my other, younger son, Leon, who was just starting to understand what all the bother was about.

When we got to the Sands, we noticed someone else waiting for the bus. On seeing us, this cheerful fellow came and introduced himself: 'Hi, I'm Colin Carter. Stuart will explain.'

Colin was a well-known figure in the Carlisle area, having been involved at one time or another with Carlisle United, the old Gretna and various other clubs. Stuart would later explain his role in the new team, initially as physio, but more importantly as a talent spotter in the amateur leagues. Full of humour and extremely passionate, Colin would often provide much-needed respite when things got a bit hectic, although he could often flare up himself. He bore more than a passing resemblance – visually as well as audibly – to the Lancastrian comedian Peter Kay, and he would soon make a habit of trudging down to the front of the bus during away trips, picking up the microphone, and proceeding to lambast various unfortunate members of the squad; members of the committee were sadly not exempt from this ridicule.

There were three members of coaching staff who would assist Stuart in that first year. In addition to Colin, there was Barry Graham, a resident of Gretna, who had known and worked with Stuart for some time. Barry, who became

Stuart's assistant manager, was a key intermediary between Stuart and the players and officials, with his cool head and calm approach. He had a unique ability to remain polite and rational in the most unreasonable of circumstances. Also helping out would be Carlisle-based Kenny Brown, another local football personality with a deadpan wit and poker face that shielded a deep intelligence and keen eye for detail.

Joining these two was Tommy Graham (no relation to Barry), also destined to be a member of the new committee, as self-declared kit man. In time the group would be joined by Megan Alexander who would soon take over as physio while Colin concentrated on coaching and scouting. Unsurprisingly none of the players seemed to object to having their aches and pains attended to by an attractive young woman.

As we entered the packed bus there was – much to our embarrassment – an outbreak of applause from the players and other travelling supporters. A number of the longer-standing fans even asked if they could have a photo of themselves with me, which I found quite humbling. There would still be a lot of work, pain, errors, decisions and arguments to come, and the glue that would hold it all together during the trickier times would be the continued commitment of the supporters.

As we drove there Stuart handed me the first ever team sheet of Gretna FC 2008. It read:

1. Stuart Pettit
2. Ross Johnston
3. Curtis Wood
4. John Jardine
5. Alex Dicker
6. Daniel Burgess
7. David Reynard
8. Daniel Rayson
9. Tony Nicholson
10. David Seggie
11. Shaun Milligan

The substitutes, all of whom would play, were John Jamieson (goalkeeper), Daniel Carmichael, Adam Mc-Math, Dean Rea, Chucky Roberts, Callum Johnstone and Teddy Harrison.

Most of the players were from Workington and were based in England (getting international clearance to play in the East of Scotland League was a bureaucratic idiosyncrasy we hadn't until then really thought about!) but a few were Scots, including Daniel Carmichael from Dumfries and Shaun Milligan who had played for the old Gretna as a youth. Goalkeeper John Jamieson's father was involved in the Fighting 46 group.

In the bus, I made a number of handwritten copies of the team sheet and handed them to some of our more vocal supporters – the idea being that our new and unknown squad would get at least some personal audible backing during the game. The idea seemed to work fairly well until late in the second half when I could clearly hear 'Oh for fuck's sake, Chucky, ma granny could've pit that wan away' when the fabulously named substitute nearly scored the new Gretna's first ever goal.

It was clear that the match would be fairly one-sided, effectively Workington's first team against their former youth side, and the final score was a 5-0 defeat for Gretna. However the result paled into insignificance compared with the occasion itself. There was certainly much to be encouraged by. Four players stood out: John Jardine in defence, David Seggie in midfield, Tony Nicholson and Daniel Carmichael up front. All four would become permanent members of the team in its first few years and Daniel Carmichael would eventually be sold to Queen of the South.

Now that we had a team, we needed to get on with sorting out the governance of the club. At our support-ers' society board meeting on the following Monday we agreed that Gretna Supporters' Society would be the owner of the club holding the initial 1,000 shares. A new company would be set up (Gretna FC 2008 Ltd) with a board (we called it a committee to distinguish it from the GSS board) to run the football club. Therefore Gretna Supporters' Society would own the club and its board would hold the Gretna FC 2008 committee to account. This set up was partly to ensure that the committee had the right sort of skills on it, especially in the early days, and was seen as a temporary arrangement. In time the GSS board would replace the committee, but back in the late summer of 2008 the board members simply lacked some of the skills and capacity needed to change from running a supporters' club to a football club.

There was some crossover. From the supporters' society board, the following were elected to the committee: Craig (who was chairman of the board), Ann Burnett, Kathryn Elliot, Ann Hipwell and myself. To this group we added Pete (to be treasurer), Sandra Bowden (as secretary), Ken Davies (health and safety) and Tommy Graham. The board asked me to become chairman of the football club committee, which I accepted with some honour, although I felt that would be temporary until we got things up and running and I could hand over to someone more local and with more history invested in Gretna.

Others were asked to help out. From the supporters' society board, Doug Branney would be the official photographer and Steve English would have responsibility for IT and communications helped by (Chorley) Tony Woffindin. We asked Helen MacGregor to advise Ann Burnett in her role as matchday secretary and Pete agreed to write to Ron and Helen to explain why we would not be asking either of them on to the new football committee. This was done in good faith, an attempt to show how the new was different from the old, but I'm afraid it backfired and upset the MacGregors who had offered us nothing but valuable support through the process. Ron and Helen were well known and highly regarded throughout Scottish football and we could have sought to emphasise the distinction between old and new in a more tactful way. It did not diminish Ron and Helen's support for the club and, nearly seven years later, they can still be found attending most games, whereas many of the original committee and board have long since departed.

Craig and Tommy agreed to take on the role of developing a youth team with Stuart, although that was not an immediate priority. Pete finalised the business plan into what was effectively our budget now. Our main costs turned out to be players' expenses. None of our players were paid – the only money they received were reimbursements for the costs they incurred travelling to training and to Raydale on match day, although a few did receive a small signing-on fee. For away games, the supporters' society laid on a coach, with the spare seats taken up by paying fans. Other costs were the rental of the Everholm, payments to referees and other officials, insurance, laundry, medical costs and other equipment costs. In our first season we ended up spending just over £25,000, of which half went to the players. The money for this came from matchday income (gate receipts of £6,000, programme net profits of £2,500), sponsorship (£5,000) and fundraising (£8,000). Donations, sales of merchandise and refreshments made up the difference. Although we always had the supporters' society money to fall back as a safety net, there was actually no need for that in our first year.

We also agreed to send a letter to Brooks Mileson – nothing ventured, nothing gained – asking about the possibility of a no-strings donation to the new club. As expected, we did not receive a reply.

Before closing the meeting, we confirmed the remaining pre-season friendlies to be held in the weeks following, before our first league game – away to Kelso United on Saturday 9 August. We beat Carlisle team Gilford Park 4-1, but lost to Dalbeattie Star and Blyth Spartans (both times 1-2). I experienced a rather disorientating conversation while on holiday, travelling on a bus travelling through Reykjavík. I answered my mobile to a call from the BBC asking for my verdict on the 4-1 victory. Someone had texted me the important details of a game I hadn't seen so I was able to wing it until, under the pressure of a bus load of fluent English-speaking Icelanders, all eyeing me with grave Nordic suspicion, I came clean and admitted where I was. Our last friendly was away to Penrith on Friday 1 August. This time we lost 4-1 despite going in front with a goal from Tony Nicholson. Man of the match that evening was Nikki White with his 'never-say-die' attitude. Nikki was also a resident of Gretna, much involved with village life, and he would go on and become an important component of the club's backbone in the years to come.

As we prepared for the trip to Kelso, Stuart rang me to say he had agreed a deal with ex-Gretna FC defender Mark Birch. Mark played at Hampden in the Scottish Cup Final in 2006 and still lived locally. A small signing-on fee was agreed but, like the others, he would not be receiving anything else besides expenses. I called Steve English on Friday afternoon and sent a press release which he placed on the website. Unfortunately, in my rush, I made a fairly glaring spelling mistake, leading to the headline 'Bitch signs for Gretna' on the web. It did not stay there for long!

The next morning, 9 August 2008, we travelled over the border in pouring rain, genuinely concerned about whether Gretna FC 2008's first league game would go ahead. For those whose experience of football is of fabulously tended and weather-resistant Premier League pitches (Motherwell's Fir Park excepted), it can be quite a shock just how much lower league fixtures are at the mercy of the elements. However, as we passed through Moss Paul – where the Scottish Borders meet Dumfries and Galloway, twenty-five miles north of Gretna, thirteen south of Hawick – the rain stopped. By the time we got to Kelso the sun was shining.

At the ground, I spoke to local radio. The interviewer reminded me that Gretna FC was soon to be liquidated, an inevitability that barely registered now. The game began with the team, solidified by Birch, not showing anywhere near the same level of nervousness as those of us in the committee. By half-time we were 1-0 up, courtesy of Daniel Carmichael. Kelso came back strongly but John Jamieson, who had established himself during the friendlies as the wearer of the number 1 shirt, made a number of excellent saves. Dean Rea came on in the second half and this galvanised the players, with Dan Rayson chipping the Kelso goalie from twenty-five yards and Carmichael getting his second to make the final score a 3-0 win.

The game looked like it would be a one-off for Mark Birch – he soon signed for Penrith, where he would receive some wages, although not before admitting that pulling on a Gretna shirt again had been a poignant moment. However, the youngsters did not seem to miss him. On the following Wednesday we travelled once again into the Borders for an evening game at Gala Fairydean, returning home with a 4-0 victory and the players singing 'Hello, Hello, We're top of the league are you're no!'

Our first home game was due to be on Saturday 16 August against Craigroyston, but after days of heavy rain, the pitch at Everholm was unplayable and Stuart took the sensible decision that it needed some respite and the game was called off. We were shocked to find out that one of Annan's teams used it on the Sunday, cutting it up further, resulting in a discussion with the Annandale and Eskdale Leisure Trust about keeping the pitch at playing standard.

The next weekend we did manage to get the game on and the day was an overall success. We spent some time going through procedures including roping off the pitch from the spectators, setting up our mini ticket office, arranging ball boys, and sorting out a process for paying the match officials and players' expenses. All went remarkably smoothly and we celebrated the 2-1 win in the Bluebell Inn, 100 metres away, where we had organised refreshments for the players. Our next games saw further victories, including 6-3 against at home to Tynecastle in the Scottish Challenge Cup, where ex-Gretna FC striker David Bingham, now player-manager at Tynecastle, scored two of their goals.

For a while it was like the season in the Premier League had never happened as a Gretna team kept winning game after game – against Selkirk, Lothian Thistle and Hawick Royal Albert. Inevitably the first defeat came, in controversial circumstances at the Everholm in the next round of the Challenge Cup on Saturday 18 October. Our opponents were Edinburgh City, who played in the East of Scotland Premier League – one tier above us. We started well, Tony Nicholson scoring to make it 1-0 at half-time. However in the fifty-fifth minute, against the run of play, an innocuous-looking clash between John Jamieson and a City player changed the game. The volcanic Gretna keeper took umbrage at being felled and hit out at his opponent. Gretna were down to ten men and facing a penalty. Despite the valiant efforts of Steven Rudd, a midfielder who pulled on Jamieson's top, City drew level. The game finished 3-1. Our supporters became very animated by the end of the game and I recall walking the referee back to the pavilion, trying (unsuccessfully) to drown out colourful verbal complaints and sending a letter of apology to Edinburgh City. We were a young team, still learning, and the response back from City was very supportive.

A couple of weeks later, the team was back to winning ways with a 5-2 victory over Kelso, a result which meant that the new Gretna would be playing in the final of the Alex Jack Cup against Tynecastle, the date scheduled for Sunday 30 November. Before that however, there was the closing of the story of Brooks Mileson.

13

Almost no one had heard from Brooks Mileson for some months now. His old football club was being liquidated, with around £2 million still owed to various businesses and individuals but, other than a quick call to Ron and Helen MacGregor in early August (during which he declaimed against the actions of the administrators), his illness continued to prevent him from engaging with anyone at Gretna or in the media. On 20 August, Carlisle United went to court seeking redress for £88,000 which Mileson had promised in sponsorship money to his former favourites. United's action was frowned upon by many observers, not least as it wasn't clear what Mileson would be getting from the deal, having already poured significant amounts into the club. Mileson did not attend court, instead sending a letter which said, 'I am unable to express myself and have problems with speech and understanding.' The judge ruled that Mileson had ten weeks to present medical evidence backing this up, otherwise he would have to appear at a rearranged date, set for Wednesday 5 November. Many others would be watching should the legal case succeed in flushing him out of hiding.

Whatever the merits of the Carlisle United case, the administrator continued to work for the creditors who were owed money by the now-liquidated Gretna FC, rather than by Mileson personally, although David Elliot's case hung on linking the two, with reference to the note in the 2005-06 accounts whereby Mileson guaranteed the club's debt until March 2008. The sum reported as owed to creditors, excluding Mileson himself, was now £2.2 million. Even any proceeds from the sale of Raydale would come nowhere close to meeting that. Elliot was now taking legal advice to see if he could go after Mileson himself.

It will never be known what strain this put on Mileson. Only a year earlier, he had declared his love for Gretna and linked his survival against various illnesses to it: 'This club is my soul. I would have ended up croaking if I had not come to Gretna.' It was the adrenaline, he said, which kept him going. Now that Gretna FC was no more, what would become of the man? The answer came on 3 November, two days before the rescheduled court hearing. On that day, Mileson's gardener, Robert Cookson, found him lying in the pond in the grounds of his house at Blackford, just outside Carlisle. Facing upwards, Mileson had collapsed, perhaps due to a heart condition, and when neither Cookson nor subsequent paramedics were unable to revive him, Brooks Mileson, age sixty-one, was pronounced dead.

The obituaries were mixed, perhaps as expected. Davie Irons called him 'one of the most generous men I've ever met in my life', refusing to be drawn into any harsh judgement. That was the cue I also took for the various media enquiries to the new Gretna club, emphasising his generosity to sports fans throughout the UK and also passing on our condolences to his family, especially Craig, who many of us knew through his involvement at Raydale. This was not the time to reopen the inquiry about what had happened to the old club – that would surely come soon enough. The strangest episode I encountered was a live interview on the pitch at Carlisle's Brunton Park, from where the local TV sports news had set up shop intending to lead on what they thought would be the headline story – the sacking of Carlisle United manager John Ward after ten defeats in the previous eleven matches.

Other tributes were paid to Mileson from up and down the country, including from Gordon Smith, the SFA Chief Executive, journalist and broadcaster Jim Traynor ('why can't we all just think of Gretna's meteoric rise and their equally dramatic fall to earth in a kinder light?') and a whole host of ex-Gretna players. However it was Gretna's demise, which even Smith had to admit in his tribute was disappointing, that would cast a long shadow over Mileson's life. Back in 2004, when Gretna were still in the Third Division, Mileson had spoken about the club's reliance on him, with no idea of what the future held for one of Scotland's biggest clubs: 'We are not Rangers or Celtic, nor will we ever be. We're just a nice, little professional club who try to do things properly. Of course *they* can't sustain themselves. Of course there is no population, but I've never walked away from anything in my life. No matter what happens, I will always make sure Gretna is looked after.'

He didn't. Whether that was a result of his illness, family pressures or anything else, we will never know, but it was a failure which ensured that his life ended with a reputation he would never have wished, and questions unanswered.

Those questions would linger on and the administrator continued his pursuit of whatever wealth remained in Mileson's name. In April 2009, at a creditors' meeting, Elliot stormed out after failing to get agreement about a percentage cut he could keep from the recovery of any further assets – his starting proposal was 20%.

Almost a year after Mileson's death, in October 2009, it was revealed that all of his supposed fortune had gone. Although his remaining assets were worth £2.5 million, his debts amounted to £8 million. This figure included the Gretna creditors (now stated as £2.5 million), unpaid income tax (£239,000), two mortgages (£614,000) and money owed to his former business partner Robert Ward, who was claiming £1.85 million. In February 2010, Mileson was finally declared bankrupt and, following a petition from Ward, proceedings were started to recover whatever assets from Mileson's family as could be found. This included the land and property at Blackford, said to be worth around £700,000, where his widow Geraldine still lived. A couple of months later, *The Scotsman* sent a journalist to the 'rundown mansion' which appeared to be deserted: 'The once stunning Japanese garden is now derelict. The large aviary, which once housed many exotic birds and the huge pond beside it – where he was found collapsed – are also empty and falling into rapid decline.'

In November 2009, there was a further meeting of Gretna creditors. Raydale had by then been sold, yet all that was left in the kitty to pay them was a meagre £715.65 – or about £5 each. The only people who got anything out of the whole sad story were those at Wilson Field, who banked £482,850 in their two and a half years as administrators and liquidators. £300,251.52 from the sale of Raydale (despite it being valued at more than twice that amount earlier in the process) had gone.

At the time of writing, this part of the tale of Gretna FC has yet to reach closure. In 2012, it was reported that Geraldine Mileson had purchased an £800,000 country house near Kendal and rumours continue that the re-mainder of Mileson's fortune is hidden away in property at home and abroad or in secret trust funds. It seems unlikely that anyone will ever get to the bottom of it all.

The administrator's pretence of utter frustration as he struggled to solve Mileson's financial puzzle left me annoyed at the time, knowing he was draining the club of its last few pennies (provided by us fans and the SPL) yet getting nowhere. I have much more sympathy for the creditors, small businesses and individuals who trusted the club to settle up but were left paying the price.

It is impossible now, with no evidence to the contrary, to conclude anything other than that the money had just run out. Perhaps the cash flow had been exaggerated. In his 2010 book, *Waste of Money: Overspending in Football*, Paul Stenning wrote that Mileson had been 'worth close to a *billion* pounds when he first purchased Gretna' but by the time he withdrew, he was 'reportedly hundreds of millions in debt'. This is an extreme example, an embellishment on both counts, but maybe the £8 million that Mileson put into Gretna was in fact a larger proportion of his wealth than we realised.

The press interest in his family seems to have receded in recent years. That is a good thing. They certainly do not appear to be living it up with ostentatious wealth. They will eternally be burdened with the black mark against the name of their father and husband for his treatment of small businesses, his reputation tarnished with the failure of his last great project. Shrewd businessmen do not always appear able to transfer their skills into the successful running – in the long term – of a football club. Yet

I hope the family will also know that many remember the philanthropy too.

For fans, it is also a mixed legacy. While it is easy to recall the great times with Mileson (and there were many, as he would say, which were 'so much fun'), it is often difficult to forgive the fact that our club was killed off. Nevertheless, we continue to move on.

A few days after his death, BBC Match of the Day cameras turned up at Gretna 2008's next match, an Image Printers Cup quarter-final tie away to Stirling University. The quality of the game itself was worthy of being shown nationally on evening television (a 3-1 win for Gretna after extra time) but the crew was there to follow up the Mileson story and the game was preceded by a minute's silence. Our players wore black armbands and the thrilling match was watched by Gavin Skelton, who came along to pay his respects too.

By the end of November, Gretna 2008 had won all five league games, but due to the number of cup games and weather-induced postponements, were sitting only third in the league. Gala Fairydean had played six more games but had only four more points, Craigroyston were in second place with sixteen points from eight games. Our good run of form had sparked the interest of Annan Athletic, who told us they were minded to approach a number of our players, notably Tony Nicholson and Daniel Carmichael.

As luck would have it, we would only play two more games that year, both defeats – in the Image Printers Cup to Edinburgh City, this time 3-2, and on 13 December, a 1-0 away defeat at Craigroyston, bringing our first loss in the league. The Alex Jack Cup Final was meant to have taken place in the midst of these defeats but, once again, the Scottish winter weather took its toll. The game was finally played on Sunday 8 January, more than five weeks after our last game.

The final was played on a neutral ground, at Galashiels, which was helpfully midway between Gretna and Edinburgh, home of our opponents, Tynecastle. Despite a 6-3 defeat by Gretna earlier in the season, Tynecastle, now led by ex-Gretna FC favourite David Bingham, had perked up recently. On the day of the game, Rufus and I were honoured to be sitting next to Bingham's old striking partner, Kenny Deuchar, who was there to file a report for *The Sun*. Despite the terrible conditions – driving rain and high winds – the game went ahead and Daniel Carmichael put Gretna into the lead on twenty-seven minutes, although that scoreline lasted only three minutes when Ross Allum equalised. After thirty-six minutes, Gretna were in the lead again courtesy of Tony Nicholson, and midway through the second half David Renyard made it 3-1. A few minutes later it was 3-2 when Darren Aird scored from the penalty spot, but David Seggie added Gretna's fourth with only ten minutes to go. By the end of the game, the players of both sides looked like they had been sharing a mud bath, but for one side at least that didn't matter. It was also nice to watch Deuchar cheer our team as each of the goals went in – genuine cheers too, reflected in his report: 'It was a privilege to watch my old club smile once more … The team got great support and I was so happy to see Gretna win the cup. For me the club is back to how it used to be before Brooks started investing heavily.'

Deuchar also revealed he had been doing his home-work: 'It's the real Gretna again. It's about people putting the time and effort in to raise money through dances and race nights … The people behind the reformed Gretna are working so hard to make sure the club carries on in a far different way.'

The celebrations continued long into the Sunday night at the social club and it was heartening to see the press coverage given to the new team which had certainly exceeded my expectations. Back in the previous summer, our desperate aim had been to get a club up and running. Any delay would have killed it off, and frankly at one stage the possibility of winning trophies would have seemed like a dream too far. However, under the leadership of Stuart and his coaches, the supporters of Gretna now had more than a team – they had a very good team – and our job on the football committee was to ensure we got back to playing in the town itself as soon as we could.

We were not able to ride on the cup success as the elements conspired to ensure our next game did not take place for another four weeks – another cup game, the King Cup, this time a 2-1 defeat at Vale of Leithen. On 21 February, Everholm finally saw its first home league game of the season in which Gretna trounced Hawick

Royal Albert 4-0, with half of the goals being scored by Hawick's debutante Colin Halfpenny, who last played four months previously in the Borders Amateur League. After the game, Halfpenny provided an honest if entertaining postscript to the match to the local newspaper, the *Southern Reporter*: 'I haven't really trained, never mind played, for weeks – and turned out for the Albert just to help out. I enjoyed the game, although I could have done without scoring the two own goals. I was a bit unlucky with the first as I got my head to a cross that would not have come my way had it not been for the wind. And for the second I just stuck out my foot to stop a shot. The ball could have gone anywhere, but it had to end up in the back of the net, didn't it?'

Gretna played well in March with four victories and sat third in the table, two points behind Tynecastle, but with two games in hand. April, however, would prove to be a bleak month. There were four league games and one final cup tie, the latter possibly providing our best display up at Preston Athletic, near the site of the Battle of Prestonpans. The football game was settled in less violent fashion by penalties when the game ended 1-1. Preston won the shootout 4-2. The league games were disappointing and Gretna had slipped to fifth place by the beginning of May.

There were now five games left and it was certainly still possible for Gretna to win the division, although realistically we were looking for promotion as runners-up. On 9 May we thumped Civil Service Strollers 5-0 and followed that up with a 3-1 victory over Vale of Leithen. A 4-0 defeat to Tynecastle enabled them to clinch the championship, which they did against nine-man Gretna, beating us 4-0. In that game both John Jardine and Nikki White were sent off, followed by goalkeeper John Jamieson, whose red card was received after the final whistle.

The next game, due two days later on Monday 18 May, Gretna's fourth in nine days, would decide which of three teams would join Tynecastle in the Premier Division next season. Despite Gretna's defeat and Civil Service Strollers' 2-0 victory over Eyemouth, it was still mathematically possible for the Black and Whites to be promoted.

Gretna or Stirling University could usurp Civil Service Strollers' second place by winning all of their remaining games, by virtue of their better goal difference. As they had to play each other – Gretna's next game was at home to Stirling University – only one could do it. A draw would mean that neither would go up. Predictably that is what happened. Gretna were 2-0 up after twenty minutes via Nicholson and Carmichael, but Stirling pulled one back by half-time and then equalised in the seventy-fourth minute. After ninety-three minutes, with both sides killing each other's seasons off, the students scored. The sting so maddened Gretna that Ryan Errington immediately ran up the park and made the scores level once again. The whistle blew and our first season ended disappointingly, missing out on promotion, although we were able to salvage some enjoyment with a 4-0 victory on the final day of the season at Ormiston.

However, despite the fourth place (I would have settled for that in any league only a few months earlier!) we had much to be proud about. We had a club, we had a good team, and assuming Stuart stayed on and continued to develop one of the youngest squads in the league, we would surely be in the top division sooner or later. Despite the hard work, the fallings out, the criticism and cynicism, we were enjoying it all. We were watching a Gretna team swathed in black and white hoops play football once more. The game against Stirling University, on a Monday evening, had attracted 263 spectators.

Just over a year earlier, the old Gretna FC won the embarrassing accolade of playing host to the lowest ever Premier League crowd of 431 in the game against Inverness Caledonian Thistle. On 2 May 2009, Gretna FC 2008 recorded an attendance of 433 for the 1-1 draw with Gala Fairydean, the record for an East of Scotland League game. The reason? Not only did we have a team playing *for* Gretna again – we now had one playing *in* Gretna: we were back at Raydale.

14

As the main tangible asset left, the administrator had been keen to sell Raydale as soon as he realised that Gretna FC would be liquidated. But we were well aware that the loss of the stadium would mean little chance of a return to football in Gretna. Back on 14 July 2008, just four days after our successful presentation to the East of Scotland League, I had written to all Dumfries and Galloway councillors ahead of a full council meeting which would be discussing the issue. I wanted them to know that we did not think of Raydale just as the home of football in Gretna, but as something much more: 'We do not expect the council simply to provide some funding to ensure that the football club continues; but as a community club, run entirely by fans, we hope we hope we can help to play a part in the sporting and leisure aspect of the regeneration of Gretna.' I also pointed out – helpfully, I hoped – that other clubs had rebuilt with the support of their local council, mentioning Telford, Scarborough and Clydebank.

The decision was not the one we were looking for, the first of a series of blows that we would endure over the coming months. As a direct result of the Fighting 46 group's challenge and intervention, the councillors were unnerved and wavered under the hope that perhaps Raydale could not legally be sold by David Elliot after all, despite the assurances he claimed he had been given. There was some reassurance and a rare complimentary email from a councillor, Jane Maitland, an independent who praised our efforts and told me not to feel down-hearted. Archie Dryburgh continued his support and noted that the council would ensure that the football pitch at Raydale would remain, under General Policy 78 (Protection of Sports Facilities and Playing Fields) of the Local Plan, as a sports and recreation facility. That didn't prevent Elliot from telling the BBC that he was looking for offers of over £500,000 from 'outside football'. The Fighting 46 group then decided on another tactic. Having persuaded the majority of the council that Raydale might be obtained without the use of taxpayers' money, the group then erected a metal barricade around the ground in a bid to prevent any more of the assets from being taken away and sold.

By the middle of August, Elliot told me in a phone conversation that he was at his wits' end. He believed that the council would have bought Raydale had it not been for the Fighting 46 challenge. His exasperation was clear – he would now, he said, be starting his own legal proceedings against the challengers and made it clear that when he won, as he expected to, the Fighting 46 group (which was still only a semi-formal congregation of individuals without any legal standing and protection) would be paying his legal costs.

I had initiated the phone call to enquire about the possibility of Gretna FC 2008 using Raydale while it remained unsold, but the frustrated Elliot was in no mood to be helpful. A few days later he served notice on the social club (which was more associated with Fighting 46 than with Gretna FC 2008) giving them until the end of September to evacuate the premises. 'Their liquor licence depends on football being played there and now that is not the case,' he claimed.

A day later, Elliot spoke to the *Cumberland News* and openly accused the Fighting 46 group of scuppering the council bid:

> There has been a lot of conjecture with people saying the administrator doesn't have power to sell the ground because it doesn't belong to the football club. It's not in dispute as far as I am concerned and interested parties have been put off because of the controversy. The ground was owned by

Gretna FC. When Mr Mileson came on board he bought the ground by paying off all the old club's debts and registering it at the Scottish Land Registry. The council expressed interest in making a bid in writing and that was well received by us, but then they didn't make a formal bid. We think the council was put off by a small faction of people.

The paper then confirmed that six offers had been made for Raydale ranging from £300,000 to £1 million.

In September, Archie Dryburgh tried again in the council chamber, following discussions earlier that month between representatives of the new football club, the social club, Fighting 46 and the two community councils (Gretna and Rigg, Springfield and Gretna Green). The discussions were held to try and bring about a consensus of the various views into one 'community partnership' which would work to raise serious funds to be used to purchase Raydale. Archie's motion noted that, as it now appeared the administrator was legally able to sell the land, he was asking the council to buy Raydale at a cost of £400,000 and give the new group four years to repay what was effectively a loan.

The motion was defeated by one vote. Local MP David Mundell was highly critical: 'The council will now be seen as one of Gretna's fair-weather friends, who were happy to share in the reflected glory of the team when it was doing well, but unwilling to step up to the mark in its hour of need.' Archie Dryburgh referred to the deal as 'pulling the guts out of the community'.

Nevertheless, the idea of a community partnership remained alive and, determined not to give up despite twice being kicked, further meetings between all parties were held. Council officers were told to provide advice and support and Elaine Murray MSP also attended one. She was encouraged by Dryburgh who was privately more confident about the ongoing potential for council support at some point. So was born, in early November, the Raydale Community Partnership (RCP), representing all groups except Fighting 46 whose members had decided, despite all the evidence about the land ownership, to continue with their own campaign.

The intention of the RCP was to work quickly to secure funds, potentially supported to some extent by Dumfries and Galloway Council, to make an offer. Each of the member groups had two representatives on its committee. Both Pete and I felt strongly that the football club needed a more local face and our two representatives were Craig and Steve English, both of whom were Gretna Supporters' Society board members. The objective was that RCP would own the land that the football ground was built on, with Gretna FC 2008 paying rent. We would also look to hire out Raydale to other parties where possible. Gordon Norman from the social club was elected as the original chair with Craig as vice-chair. Frank Baillie, a colleague of Pete and myself from Cumbria County Council and a member of the social club, would be treasurer, while Kate Nutt from the Annandale and Eskdale Council for Voluntary Service would act as company secretary.

We heard little – which was welcome – from the administrator, and it wasn't until the last day of January 2009 that the next blow landed via an article in the Dumfries Standard: 'Dreams were shattered in Gretna this week when it was revealed out of the blue that Raydale Park is about to be sold.' Craig Peacock, a local councillor and member of the RCP board spoke on behalf of the partnership, expressing his shock. RCP had recently approved a three-year business plan and, having made contact with the administrator, was awaiting a reply from him.

Once again we had to pick ourselves up off the ground, brush away the dust and continue. If Raydale really was on the point of being sold, this did not necessary mean all was lost. Our hunch was that it would be attractive to a potential property developer, particularly if linked up with land to the west of the town, and with any prospective buyer aware of the local planning issues and General Policy 78 (as they certainly would be) we might be able to save the football pitch and accompanying facilities.

We had no idea who the buyer was, if indeed there was one; we were growing increasingly suspicious of the administrator's pronouncements and games. We had looked at using some land in nearby Springfield, but its low quality had led to it being ruled out. With rumours rife in the small town – it was impossible to do pretty much anything without someone seeing it, so the chances of an inspection of a public park not being reported throughout the locality were fairly slim – I felt the need to be open about the developments in the programme notes for our game on 7 March. We knew the outcome would be disappointing to some of our supporters who were growing tired of the trips to Annan for home games.

In the end, it was Stuart Rome who again came to the rescue of the club and found the key which unlocked the door to a meeting with the buyer of Raydale. I've never been entirely clear how that happened (I'm not sure I wanted to know – or cared – at the time) but on Easter Monday, Stuart picked up a wealthy property developer, Raydale's new owner, from Carlisle Airport and drove him to a hotel on the outskirts of Gretna where Craig Williamson, Pete and myself were waiting. After a number of setbacks over the previous months, our guest, representing a company called Sawtry (IOM) Ltd but insisting on secrecy at that stage, now offered us a lifeline. Sawtry was not interested in the football park itself but, pending some planning permission approvals, were looking at a much bigger project, having purchased the old golf course just to the west. It would eventually lead to an application being lodged with the planning authority in October that year, but for now our guest was willing to sell Raydale back to us for £320,000 as long as we could raise the money by 1 May 2010. Between now and then, we were expected to be supportive of his larger plans but could use Raydale as soon as we were able to. We would lease the ground off him during that year for a nominal fee of £1.

We were understandably ecstatic and immediately began work on getting back to our spiritual home. Although we would need a few more equally clandestine meetings before all the details were finalised, we felt confident enough to issue a press release a few days later on Friday 17 April:

> There has been much speculation in the community in recent weeks concerning the sale of Raydale. It has now been confirmed that the land has been sold to a developer who wishes to improve and increase housing and facilities in the town.
>
> Over the past few weeks, the Raydale Community Partnership has been in discussion with the new owner of Raydale and hopes to be able to finalise a deal in the next few days which will safeguard the future of the social club, the Sunday market, and allow Gretna FC 2008 to play matches at Raydale as soon as this is physically possible.
>
> The Raydale Community Partnership is an incorporated company constituted by Gretna FC 2008, the Gretna Social and Athletic Club, Gretna and Rigg Community Council and Gretna Green Community Council. The partnership will enter into an agreement with the new owner which will result in Raydale being leased to it for one year, with immediate effect. During that period, the partnership will be seeking to raise funds to purchase the land from the new owner. The partnership is supportive of the new owner's plans for the land to the west of Raydale and believes this will improve the community.
>
> Plans are well underway to bring the football pitch up to playing standard, and more details will be released soon regarding the work required. However it is hoped that the club will be playing at Raydale later this season in its final push for promotion from the East of Scotland Football League One.

We meant what we said about timescales. We had four home games left that season: the first, on Saturday 18 April, was clearly not going to be possible, but we set our sights on the one after that, two weeks later on 2 May against Gala Fairydean. It was a tall order – the place had been pretty much left abandoned for over a year and the administrator's men had left it looking like a crime scene after a burglary, with debris of the past strewn across every available piece of floor space. The dressing rooms were filthy and untidy; a pile of UEFA cup programmes lay hidden under a dust-covered mess of old tracksuit tops and shin pads. The toilets had remained unofficially in use with visitors to the Sunday market somehow getting in and relieving themselves. Unfortunately none of those who had taken advantage of the lax security had felt any duty to come back with mops and detergent, leaving the place smelling fairly rank.

The main problem was the state of the pitch which had grown into a real meadow, lush except in those areas where hungry crows had ripped it to shreds. Work began with an army of volunteers under the leadership of Colin Cronie and Tommy Graham and the invaluable advice of Stuart and the other coaches. We also sought and were given the guidance and support of the local council, fire brigade, police and utility companies. A number of local firms also gave us favourable deals on the equipment needed to sort the place out.

Whilst this work was underway, there was a meeting of the Gretna FC creditors with the administrator on

22 April. Malcolm Dunn was unable to attend and Pete George went in his place. At the meeting, David Elliot confirmed that Raydale had been sold to Sawtry (IOM) Ltd for £300,000 – the difference in the price we had been offered was due to an extra £12,500 stamp duty plus £7,500 legal costs. The administrator also said that he had sold the Corries Stand for an extra £30,000 although contractors had not been prepared to take it down due to local opposition – it seemed the Fighting 46 campaign had produced something positive at last. Sawtry Ltd disputed the sale of the stand claiming that it was part of their deal – a fight which the administrator would eventually lose. Elliot also confirmed that he would now be pursuing Brooks Mileson's estate.

By Thursday 23 April, the grass at Raydale had been cut and watered, the changing rooms cleared and cleaned, and a plan was in place to ensure that the electricity and water would be safe. We notified the League that we intended to play at Raydale on 2 May.

We made that first Saturday in May a bit of a party by handing out some free flags and old Gretna footballs that had been left lying around. The result was disappointing – a 1-1- draw – but the party continued on late into the night at the social club. Net takings at the match were boosted by a record crowd off 433 to £2,122.25. The normal figure at the Everholm was around £380. Our last two home games of the season were also played at Raydale, with 233 supporters seeing us thrash Civil Service Strollers 5-0 on 9 May, before the disappointing but thrilling 3-3 draw against Stirling on 18 May in front of 263 spectators.

The first season was ending, but the renewal of Gretna as a football club was only just beginning. There would need to be a huge effort over the summer to get a still sick Raydale back to full health, not to mention negotiations with the new owners to reach a more permanent solution. The team had done very well in its first year but Stuart, Barry, Colin and Kenny were already on with planning for the following season. The previous twelve months had been exciting, exhilarating, draining and at times fractious. A number of members of the supporters' society board and football committee (a governance arrangement which was proving to be more cumbersome than first intended and which we needed to tidy up) had resigned either through disagreement or due to the toll it was taking on their health. Nevertheless, despite all the obstacles, we had succeeded. In my final Chairman's Chat I was keen to ensure that I thanked as many people as possible for the hard work and diligence which had got us to where we were.

> One man has done more than anything to get our club up and running, playing well and, of course, getting us back to Raydale. Stuart Rome is that man, and he deserves a medal for what he has done. Stuart is a hard-working, clear-thinking, determined and very honest man. Without him Gretna 2008 would not be what you see and cheer on today and I hope we can all make that clear at the end of tonight's game, whatever the result.

Stuart has been ably assisted by coaches and we owe Barry, Colin and Ken a debt of gratitude too. There are many others who deserve a mention too. We would be lost without Sandra's organisation skills and sheer hard work, Pete's financial acumen, Tommy and Colin Cronie's ground skills, Doug's camera and the hard work put in by those on the supporters' society board, especially Bill, John, Lynn, Ed and Alex who are always willing to help out whenever they can. We should also remember the contributions made by former members, especially Steve, Kat, Ann Burnett and Ann Hipwell. There are others too, not on the committee or board who have helped immeasurably: Morag, Margaret, Jacqueline, Alison, Ian and Jock to name just a few. I want to thank them all and many others who have got us to where we are today with their hard work, all of which is voluntary – actually, more than voluntary as they have often spent their own money in helping us.

I want to thank you the fans too for all you have done, especially those I have not mentioned (the list would fill the programme!). Finally a special word should go to Craig Williamson who puts as much time and effort into Gretna 2008 as many of us combined. His negotiating skills and ability to chair the board, sometimes in times of adversity, are another example of how the club relies on more than just one individual to keep us going. Craig and Stuart are our representatives on the Raydale Community Partnership and are leading the way in our very exciting plans for the future.

As for Raydale itself? In October the owners (now listed as Greenbank (IOM) Ltd) suffered a setback when their consent for planning permission was refused. This would have created residential housing and a new nursing home, but was turned down as 'the council as Planning Authority is not satisfied that there is sufficient need at present'. The owners made it clear they intended to try again.

By the end of the 2009-10 season, with Raydale Community Partnership still not having generated the funding to buy the ground and with the housing plans still uncertain, the owner graciously extended the lease for another year. On 6 April 2011, Dumfries and Galloway Council finally came good and awarded the RCP not a loan, but a grant of £150,000 to contribute to the purchase. A bank loan would be required for the remainder, but with half of the money secured and with the partnership up and running for eighteen months and therefore a stronger and more robust entity, such a loan became ever more feasible.

Greenbank was awaiting the final results of their planning application on the old golf course site, which came on 13 April 2011. The Planning Committee refused the application and effectively killed the proposed development. Within two months, RCP had secured the loan and purchased the entire site for a reduced price of £270,000. Raydale now belonged to Gretna once again.

15

Over the next few seasons, Gretna FC 2008 consolidated their standing in the East of Scotland League, a task which required work both on and off the field. In the summer of 2009, Raydale Park was subjected to both deep surgery and a fundamental facelift; a band of volunteers with paintbrushes, bin liners, hammers, nails, screwdrivers and whatever else it took were in on most days as we got the pitch ready for pre-season friendlies. These would include promising displays against Penrith (a 2-0 win for Gretna) and Queen of the South (a 0-0 draw). We also played our first game against the neighbours who had shared so much of Gretna's history: Annan Athletic, when a strong performance by Gretna was not enough to prevent a 1-0 defeat.

Stuart's young team was growing up, boosted by the presence of more experienced players such as Mark Birch, back for a second visit, and Simon Ruddick, who had joined the previous February and marked an unfortunate debut with an own goal against Tynecastle. A youth team was also formed, although this would eventually prove too demanding on the new club.

Off the field, we held our AGM on 25 August and presented accounts which showed that the cost of running the club in its first year had been under £25,000. Costs would grow substantially in season two following the decision to award modest win bonuses to the players: £25 each for that day's squad. This issue had consequences as Pete sadly resigned, no longer feeling certain that the club would break even. However, Stuart argued strongly – and I supported him – that if the club wished to attract the best talent in the area, there would have to be some financial consequence. We were still a long way off from paying wages, however small, and nor were we slipping back into the 'old' Gretna habit of pursuing victory at any cost. But we did recognise that we were only capable of taking players from a small north Cumbrian/Borders pool where other clubs were offering better financial incentives, which we did not even attempt to match. To ensure that costs were met, a separate players fund was set up with fundraising events organised. The most successful of these were sportsman's dinners featuring guest speakers such as Jan Molby and Howard Kendall, often bringing in profits of over £3,000 despite the best attempts of some of the speakers to drink the bar dry. If the players were very successful on the pitch, the supporters' society, which had a healthy bank balance, stood ready to bankroll any shortfall. We agreed that the player bonuses would be a one-year experiment. In the end, the society did not have to pay anything, although it did cover the cost of another expense – signing-on fees of just under £5,000.

At the AGM we also agreed new governance arrangements for the club, effectively merging the supporters' society board and the football club committee. It was my cue to step back a little – my role as chair was obsolete but I remained on the board, with Craig continuing as chairman of the new, merged board. As it happened, things didn't quieten down as expected: over the rest of the season I picked up Pete's treasurer and programme production roles, turning up at Stuart's house or Newton Rigg College near Penrith (which we used for winter training) with bags of cash and cheques for the players and coaches. John Bowden took over the finance role in the summer of 2010. By that stage I had left the board altogether, a consequence of moving to North Yorkshire with my new job.

During the 2009-10 season we became involved in the first discussions that were taking place about a potential pyramid system in Scottish football, while work continued to ensure we remained at Raydale. We were gradually creating an identity for Gretna football, although from time to time there would be the odd event which reminded us of the past. One of the oddest of these was a report in November 2009 in the best-selling national *Sunday Post* about our 3-0 victory over St Cuthbert's Wanderers which began, with stark capital letters: 'GRETNA BROKE played St Cuthbert's Wanderers for the first time…'

A gremlin or deliberate jibe? We never found out, our request for an explanation remaining unanswered.

By the end of the season we finished fourth again – Stirling University and Vale of Leithen were promoted and Craigroyston finished third. Our record was almost identical to the previous year – thirteen wins, four draws and five defeats (compared with thirteen wins, five draws and four defeats in our first season) – but this time we reached two cup finals: the Image Printers Cup, beating Vale 2-1 in the final, then losing 2-0 to Berwick Rangers in the East of Scotland (City) Cup.

After that I saw less of the club, living over 100 miles away across the border and the Pennines, although I visited when I could. The team won the First Division title the following season with a title decider against Leith Athletic in Edinburgh on 14 May – only one day adrift from being the fifth anniversary of the Scottish Cup Final and the third anniversary of Gretna FC's last ever game and Gavin Skelton's last-minute goal. On that sunny day in Leith, the youngsters from the border won 5-2.

In our first season in the East of Scotland Premier Division Gretna achieved a respectable mid-table finish (sixth of twelve) but failed for the first time to take home any silverware. The greater sadness was for the loss of Stuart Rome, the man who built the new club from scratch, but who could not ignore the call of Queen of the South. Kenny Brown took over as coach and led the team to fourth place in 2012-13. There were two trophies going back to Gretna as well that season. After beating Stirling University 2-1 in the final of the Image Printers Cup, the team made sure this time round to win the City Cup, defeating Berwick Rangers 4-2.

In June 2013, the Scottish Lowland Football League was created as part of a major shake up of how football was organised in Scotland, an outcome of the pyramid discussions we had been involved in way back in 2009. A natural companion to the better known Highland League, Gretna FC 2008 applied and was one of the twelve successful clubs to be admitted. Now playing at a much higher profile (the league has its own pages on the BBC Sport website and is featured in a number of the national newspapers), the club finished seventh in a first season where there would be no promotion or relegation. From 2014-15 the league winners have the chance to gain promotion to the new Scottish Professional Football League Two – the team finishing top of the league will play the winners of the Highland League over two legs and the victors of that contest will play a 'winners take all' two-leg game against the team which finished bottom of Scottish League Two.

So the route is clear, but can our new Gretna club ever get back there? In 2014-15, Gretna improved on the previous season, finishing third but not quite making the grade. It is a prize worth going for and is certainly achievable, as long as it happens hand in hand with a sustainable business plan. In time, with the new structure, some excellent business acumen at the club, newly acquired SFA membership and a growing number of supporters willing to lend a hand, the club will find the right level for itself.

Football has been around in Gretna for over a century and there has been a successful club there since 1946. However, as we found out back in 2008, its continued existence, like that of so many clubs, can sometimes hang by a thin and fraying thread. Without the continued support of the community, that thread will break. Thankfully, support exists in Gretna and beyond through people like Craig Williamson, Sandra Bowden, Stuart Rome (who returned as manager in summer 2014) and many others in the community too numerous to mention. It is to them that I dedicate this book and hope that it serves as a testament to their belief and hard work.

Gretna FC

Season	Division	Position	Points
1982-83	NFL1	2	60
1983-84	NFL1	8	49
1984-85	NFL1	6	59
1985-86	NFL1	11	50
1987-88	NFL1	7	57
1988-89	NFL1	3	73
1989-90	NFL1	2	75
1990-91	NFL1	1	95
1991-92	NFL1	1	85
1992-93	NPL1	6	63
1993-94	NPL1	10	55
1994-95	NPL1	11	55
1995-96	NPL1	12	52
1996-97	NPL1	16	50
1997-98	NPL1	15	48
1998-99	NPL1	12	58
1999-00	NPL1	19	40
2000-01	NPL1	16	48
2001-02	NPL1	7	63
2002-03	SFL3	6	45
2003-04	SFL3	3	68
2004-05	SFL3	1	98
2005-06	SFL2	1	88
2006-07	SFL1	1	66
2007-08	SPL	12	13

Scottish Cup: runners-up 2005-06

Gretna FC 2008

Season	Division	Position	Points
2008-09	EoS1	4	44
2009-10	EoS1	4	43
2010-11	EoS1	1	58
2011-12	EoSP	6	33
2012-13	EoSP	4	34
2013-14	Lowland	7	31
2014-15	Lowland	3	45

Alex Jack Cup: winners 2008-09, runners-up 2009-10, 2011-12
Image Printers Cup: winners 2009-10, 2012-13
East of Scotland City Cup: winners 2012-13
Lowland League Cup: runners-up 2014-15

Also from Chequered Flag Publishing:

ORIENTATION

by Adam Michie

Spurs fan Adam Michie is fed up with the Premier League. Countless television hours are devoted to it and billions of pounds are spent on players. Ticket prices have rocketed, matches are hyped beyond reality and results are predictable.

Something is missing. The soul of football has been lost.

In search of the honest roots of the sport, Adam adopted Leyton Orient in League One. Swapping Spurs' Champions League exploits in Madrid and Milan for Orient's scraps with Brentford and Bournemouth, this is the side of football where the Premier League is a distant dream and financial solvency is an achievement to be proud of.

ORIENTATION follows one ordinary football supporter trying to rediscover what it was that first made him fall in love with football.

INNOVATIVE AND EXCITING SPORTS BOOKS

Chequered Flag
PUBLISHING

www.chequeredflagpublishing.co.uk